Write That Book!

Michael Heppell

Write That Book

How to Write, Publish & Sell Your Book

Write That Book

A CIP catalogue record of this book is available from the British Library.

First edition published in the UK by Gloop Books, 2023

ISBN: 978-1-8381613-1-6 (Hardcover)
ISBN: 978-1-8381613-2-3 (Hardcover KDP Amazon)
ISBN: 978-1-8381613-3-0 (Paperback)
ISBN: 978-1-8381613-4-7 (eBook)
Imprint: Gloop Books
Typeset Matthew J Bird

For further information about this book, please contact the author at:
www.WriteThatBook.co.uk

For

Sarah Elizabeth Proctor Heppell

Thank you for making me the proudest father
and for 30 years of pure joy

Contents

Introduction

Today I'm wearing a dark blue t-shirt and printed on it, in an old-fashioned typewriter font, is this quote:

> It's not the book you read that will change your life.
>
> It's the book you write.

Over 75% of people say they want to write a book. They have a story or a message they wish to share and would like to see published. And yet, less than 1% of people fulfil that dream and see their words in print.

I want to change that. I'd like to demystify the world of writing for you and instead give you the tools you need to write, publish and sell your own book.

The feeling when you first see your book in print is extraordinary. I've heard new authors describe it as their greatest achievement. It's emotional, deeply satisfying and a feeling that will stay with you for the rest of your life.

And your book will exist long after you've gone.

With WriteThatBook.co.uk I've coached thousands of new, and experienced, authors on the 'how-to's' and the 'what's needed' to take their ideas and transform them, step-by-step, into a real book.

Now it's your turn.

But there's something else. The elephant in the room. The great unsaid among authors.

'What if I'm not good enough?'

That's where this is more than a step-by-step guide to writing a book. It will also provide you with much-needed motivation, empathy, positivity and self-confidence. I know I can do this for you because that's been my job for the last 30 years. I've written 8 personal development books, including a Sunday Times No.1 Best Seller. Books that have been used by everyone from business leaders to popular TV presenters, famous footballers to fractious families. I know how to give you all the confidence you'll need to write, publish and sell your book. And it starts now with...

1

10 Reasons Why You Should Write That Book

There are many reasons to write your book and you need to find yours. Strong emotional motivations are 'the why' that will keep you going when you'd like to stop. They're the fuel that keeps your energy levels high when a cup of tea in front of the TV feels preferable. The oomph that keeps you glued to your first draft when a part of you wants to quit.

Here are 10 reasons why I think you must write your book.

1. **Your Legacy**
2. **Fill a gap**
3. **Become better at writing**
4. **Develop your imagination**
5. **It's fun!**
6. **To entertain**
7. **Change lives**
8. **Best business card ever**
9. **You become more interesting**
10. **Accomplishment**

10.5 It makes you better

And now that list in a little more detail.

Your Legacy

Long after you and I have passed on, your book will remain. No one can take that from you. What you do in your day-to-day life will eventually be forgotten, but your book is forever. As yet unborn family members will know that their great, great ancestor wrote a book. It will be real, printed and a wonderful physical memory. You can do that.

Fill a Gap

You know that feeling you experience when you see someone else publishing their book? That doesn't happen to everyone; only to those people, like you, who have a longing to write a book of their own. It's an unfulfilled hole and it gets bigger the longer you leave it. Triggers, like opening your local paper and seeing a first-time author surrounded by their newly launched book, bring mixed emotions. Happy for them, but what about me? When will it be my turn? That's the gap and once it's filled you can feel whole again.

Become Better at Writing

The best way to become better at anything is through immersion. Writing a book does that. You'll find the time you didn't know you had, create ideas you didn't know existed and become better at writing in the process.

Your Christmas cards will pique with personality, a quarterly report will flow and I pity the person on the receiving end of your complaint letter. Yes, you'll become better at writing *everything* because you're writing your book.

Develop Your Imagination

Which is the biggest nation in the world? It's not America or China - it's your imagination! Cheesy but true. Your neural pathways are about to go into overdrive. Your best idea hasn't been thought of yet... but it's coming and your imagination is about to receive its booster.

When you write, whether it's epic adult fiction or process-driven business methodology, your imagination will accelerate. And here's the best bit; your brain won't know that you've taken a break from writing and gone on to do something else. It keeps being creative. You'll find solutions to problems that have been bugging you for years.

It's Fun!

Yes, it's infuriating and at times frustrating, but I promise you'll have fun during this process. There'll be moments when you laugh out loud and others when you have an internal giggle which will keep your spirits up. I wonder if I could encourage you to share these moments with others who are interested in and who support your endeavours. If you'd like to join my community of merry writers, visit WriteThatBook.co.uk and you'll find a group ready to support you on your journey.

To Entertain

You know when you're enjoying a book so much that you find yourself muttering the cliché, 'I couldn't put it down'; that's what your book will do. Whether it's a children's short story that leaves the young reader demanding, 'again! again!' or a moving memoir that makes the reader gasp as they relive the author's story - authors entertain.

Change Lives

Book reviews with the phrase 'life-changing' give the author a warm fuzzy feeling that goes deep into their soul. Often, it's changing the life of a person you haven't met and probably never will. Your story can do that. If that isn't a good enough reason to put pen to paper, I'm not sure what is.

Best Business Card ever

If you own a business, you're ambitious or you want to be known as an expert in your field, then writing and publishing a book is a game changer. You'll instantly propel yourself to the top of your field and that increases your value. Authority has Author in it. Writing a book could be your best business card ever, but there's a caveat. It must be a good book and it has to be marketed. And I'll help you with that.

You Become More Interesting

Imagine being invited to a friend's party. You're introduced to a small group and the usual 'What do you do?', conversation takes place. One person says, 'I've just published my first book.' Who gets the most follow-up questions? People are interested in authors because they are interesting people. And when you've written your book, you'll have a mine of information ready to share. It might be an opportunity to sell a few books, too!

Accomplishment

Writing a book is a huge accomplishment. It's right up there with climbing the highest mountains and completing mega triathlons. There will be ups and downs, moments of joy and times of despair, but it's all worth it. Your name, on the front of your book and you wrote it. Not a ghostwriter. Not a friend. You. You can keep your Kilimanjaro! You'll have written your own book.

It Makes You Better

The process of writing your book will make you a better person. Over the last thirty years, I've coached thousands of people who want to be better. Nothing improves you like writing a book. You develop time-management, creativity and organisational skills. Your confidence increases, you learn to sell yourself (I know that sounds scary right now) and you might become a technical whizz. Plus, I promise you'll become a more proficient and faster typist.

Are you still up for this? Of course you are. Read on and I'll show you ...

2

How To Use This Book

Most ‘how to’ books are frustrating and some quite boring.

I think this could be because the self-indulgent author thinks the reader needs to read everything. Then organises their book in such a way that the learner must wade through the entire book to get to the knowledge they want.

I don’t want you to do that. I’ve designed Write That Book so you can jump around and head straight to the bits you need when you need them. Please use this book as a reference; if you want to start with the 'sell' elements, go for it. If you're interested in knowing how to pitch a publisher on day one, do it.

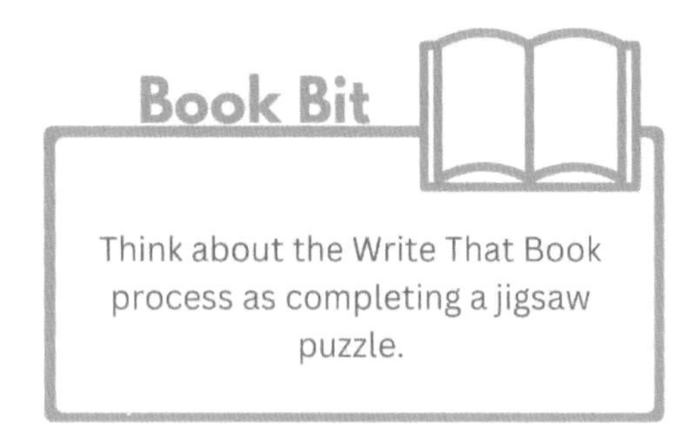

Most dissectologists* complete jigsaws in the same way. They start by turning all the pieces the right way while scanning for the edges and the four corners. Once the corners are found they’re put in place and the straight edges are completed. Now you know how big the jigsaw is going to be and the space you’re working in.

*Who knew a dissectologist is someone who completes jigsaws?

And finally, colours are coherent, faces identified, patterns matched and like pieces linked.

Initially, completing a 1,000-piece jigsaw puzzle is slow going - but you accept that. Then, part way in, the pace increases. Late nights end with 'just one more piece' and you're on a mission. You're determined to finish the puzzle.

This is the same with Writing, Publishing and Selling your book. The start might be a little disjointed, but by using this book you will see the picture form, the pieces fit together and experience the rush of getting your book over the line.

The four corners of the Write That Book jigsaw are; your idea, writing, marketing & tribe building and publishing.

Like the jigsaw, you need all four corners.

The next phase is to complete those outer edges. This is the framework that you're going to work within. When children first start to explore jigsaws, they don't begin with a 2,000-piece, reverse-cut mindbender. They play with simple two or four-piece puzzles. You're going to do the same. There will be simple parts and there will be more complex pieces. Obviously, completing the complex sections bring the biggest thrills, but it's the simple pieces that give you the momentum to keep going.

When you set out to complete a jigsaw puzzle, you don't start at the top left and fill in each piece until you get to the bottom right. It's a holistic, creative, process.

It's the same with this book. Use it as a resource to suit your needs. Write in the margins. Add Post-It notes. Use it as a guide, a friendly support to help you to write, publish and sell your book.

You'll notice the order of the three main sections. Write, Publish and Sell is changed to Write, Sell and Publish. Has he gone mad? It will make more sense as you read on and take action.

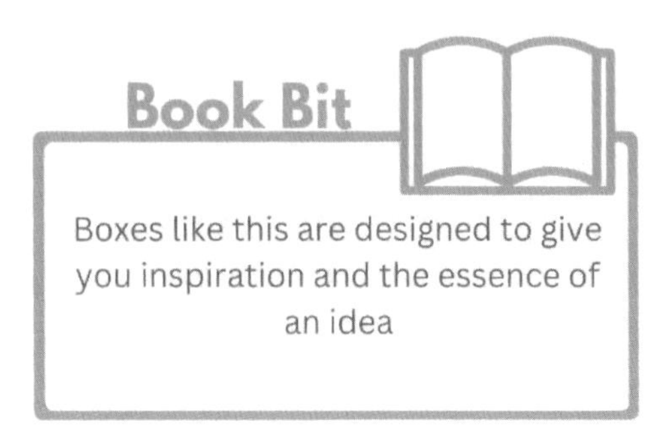

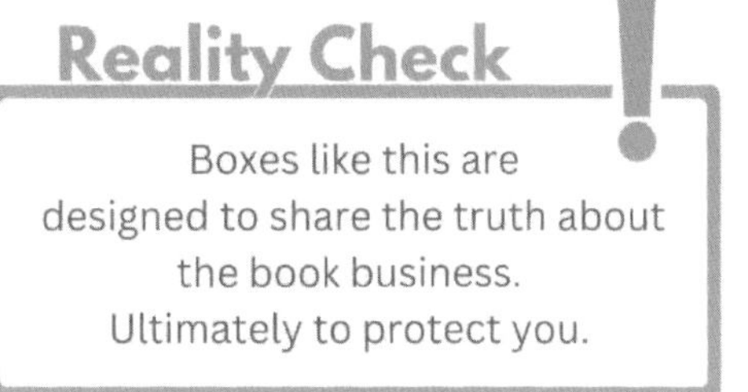

So where to begin? I suggest you start with...

3

Your Brilliant Idea

What's your book about?

Before you answer the question that all authors are asked, I want you to take one step back and consider a deeper question.

In these pages, I'm going to refer to my online Write That Book programmes. I've coached thousands of people through them, so it makes sense to take that learning and put it here.

When I run a course, the first task I give everyone isn't to share what you're writing about, it's to **post your passion.** That's because I'm more interested in what an author has as their driver in life rather than what they're going to write about.

What's your passion?

Reality Check!

Unless you're passionate about your subject, you will likely quit the writing process before you've completed your book.

I'm a super positive person, so talking about quitting doesn't feel good to me. But having taught thousands of new authors how to write their books, I know that the ones who see it through all have the spark and a passion for their subject.

If you think you should be writing a book about dragons and fairies, but your passion is pivot tables and spreadsheets (probably the other way around) maybe you should rethink your idea.

During this process, there are going to be lots of ups and downs. I call it the Author-Coaster and you'll ride it in Chapter 4. During those difficult times, it will be your passion that ensures you keep going and write your book.

Although ideas are important, good ideas are like tummy buttons - everyone's got one. It's the execution of the idea that's important. What makes your idea special? It doesn't have to be original. But it does have to be special.

I might suggest you shouldn't have an original idea. There are very few that are completely original. And this is okay. Your reader would rather have familiarity than uniqueness. It can be too much for our wonderful brains to concentrate on pages peppered with original ideas.

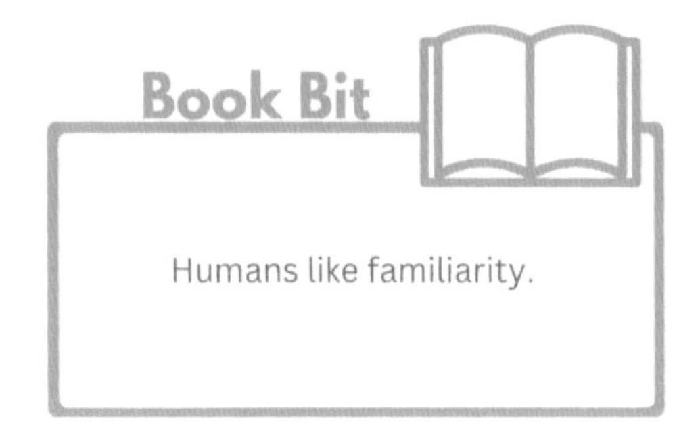

A great example of this is Owen Maclaren's invention of the fold-up pushchair. You've seen them, they pack small, fit in the boot of any car and expand to toddler size in seconds. You've probably used one.

But to introduce such a unique idea and to have consumers accept it, needed some smart thinking. The main aesthetic feature Mr Maclaren added was to manufacture the pushchairs with thick blue and white stripes. You can probably visualise a Maclaren pop-up pushchair now. And without too much additional thinking you can also visualise ... a deck chair.

Maclaren knew their potential customers were familiar with the setting up of a deck chair; but you can imagine their focus groups found parents who were unsure about the idea of a 'collapsible' pushchair? This was the age of the Silver Cross baby carriage.

Let's go back to your idea.

Here are 10 questions to consider when developing your idea:

1. **What's your passion?**
2. **Who has had a similar idea? Remember, this isn't a bad thing.**
3. **What makes your idea special?**
4. **Can you describe your idea in one sentence?**
5. **Do you believe in this idea enough to spend the time Writing, Publishing and Selling your book?**
6. **What would take this from a good idea to a great one?**

7. **Does your idea keep you awake at night - it should.**
8. **Could you write three books on this (even if you only plan to write one)?**
9. **What would the first follow-up question someone would ask when you share your idea?**
10. **Is your idea commercial?**

Now I've got your braining buzzing let's mix it up even more with a ride on...

4

The Author-Coaster

I'd like to offer you a ticket for the Author-Coaster. Anybody who has ever written seriously has taken this ride. Are you ready? You've bought your ticket and now it's time to get on board!

How did it feel the first time you climbed aboard a roller coaster? Excitement mixed with fear and a wedge of doubt? You *think* you'll be safe; there's a restraint that comes over your head or around your waist - click. Then the roller coaster leaves the station and you're committed. There's no getting off.

It's the same as writing. You commit, 'Yes, I will write a book. I'm going to write a book' Then just like the ride, the first wedge of doubt. Do I have to go up there? It didn't look quite so high from the ground. You look ahead at the track and the chain pulling the carriage skyward.

Click, click, click, the roller coaster climbs. Do you remember that moment, the feeling when you're being pulled up, up, up? That's a good time, you're excited, can still talk and you don't have to do anything other than sit tight and wait.

> 'I have a good idea'. Click click.
> 'I want to write a book'. Click click.
> 'I am going to write a book'. Click click.
> 'Yep. I'm definitely writing my book'. Click...

Now you're at the top, the wind whistles, the carriage pauses and then it's time. Time for the first drop. Whoosh! Now you're what's known as obligated. Just like the carriage must let the laws of gravity take control, you must write. Prove that you can write. While simultaneously thinking, 'Oh my goodness, the last time I seriously wrote anything was years ago and now I have to write a boooooook!' The wedge of doubt is still there, but you're off! After the first couple of dips, you catch your breath and start to enjoy it. Actually, this IS good. I MUST do this. I CAN do this.

You decide to share your journey and put it out there. After all, riding the Author-Coaster will be better with friends cheering you on.

The first person you show your writing to likes it. The second, a family member, is equally impressed. 'Wow, you're a good writer!'

Your confidence soars. This Author-Coaster is great! Then you give your work to someone you admire; they take a look and ask if you'd like their 'honest opinion'. Two words an author doesn't want to hear are 'honest' and 'opinion'. And even though their honest opinion is sugar-coated, you can feel the criticism, and worse, the accuracy of it.

Is this worthwhile? Should I bother? Whoosh!

You have a word with yourself and decide what the heck, I'm going to get a publisher or an agent - somebody who can help me. You do your research to see what the right fit for your work will be and again there's a surge of excitement. You peruse Twitter and LinkedIn and start making connections. You have your hit list. It's time, now or never, to send out your pitch.

The first response comes back quickly - literally within a few hours. However, their message is short and simple. They don't represent people who write in this genre. Oh well...

The next appears and it's... positive! They'd love to publish your book. OMG! And all you have to do is shell out a mere £20,000, for which they'll write a press release and print 100 copies. Nope, not for you.

The third is an outright rejection, as is the fourth ... the fifth ... and the sixth. How many rejections did JK Rowling receive? 'What's the point?' you say, 'Perhaps I'm not a writer after all. Does this Author-Coaster only go down?'

Then one more response. Although it is another rejection at least this one has some feedback - and feedback is useful. They say you've 'written some really good content' and they'd 'like to see a future version'. There's hope!

You keep writing; you write every day and it feels good. The Author-Coaster is at full speed - you're enjoying this last part of the ride. Then suddenly the brakes lock and with a screech you're back at the boarding station. With a choice...

Do you stay on and continue to experience the Author-Coaster? Or play it safe and take a ride on the carousel? It's easy and gentle. But carousel riders don't become writers. They don't get to hold their book and say, 'I wrote that'.

Every writer has been on the Author-Coaster. Actually, every writer is still on the Author-Coaster! It's up and down, it's fast and slow, sometimes thrilling often terrifying but never dull. You've bought your ticket, you're holding it... might as well enjoy the ride.

It's your new job. Your new primary focus in life. It's called...

Write That Book

5

Read, Write, Edit, Repeat

This is my mantra for successfully getting your book over the line. There is no doubt that these four words are the silver bullet, the magic wand and the secret sauce.

Repeat the process over and over and you will write your book.

Read

Let's start with reading. 'But Michael. I thought this was Write That Book, not Read That Book.'

I know, I too could be tempted to subscribe to that thinking. Making the time to read while you're desperately looking for the time to write is tough. However, the more I study successful authors, the more I realise they have one overriding habit; they all read every day. They also write every day, but more about that in a moment.

The way authors read is a little different from normal readers. They have concurrent trains of thought.

One is to enjoy the book. Just like everyone else, they love a good yarn, to learn something new, to add to their existing knowledge.

They also spend time thinking about what they've just read. If they enjoy a turn of phrase, they'll make a note in the margin or stick a mini Post-It note onto a page. I, like many authors, make sure I read with a pen in hand.

I used to make notes in books, but now I've progressed to taking pictures of pages and filing them for easy access to the information when I need it. Your smartphone does that too.

When I reach the end of a book, I'll review it and often add to my notepad the things I've enjoyed about it. By the time I've read it, made notes, taken pictures and copied the notes, the stand out details are usually memorable. But if not, then I know where to find them. And invariably, by going back over my notes, I'll find something else which is an added bonus!

You also improve your vocabulary, discover clever plot structures and learn smart descriptors from reading brilliant authors. There is no doubt that part of their talent flows into you as you read their words.

And, as a writer, this is part of the job. You learn by doing something you love.

Write

Great authors write every day. Good authors write most days. Average authors write when they can. If you'd like to describe yourself as a writer, start by writing every day. It doesn't mean you're writing your book every day, but it does mean you're spending some time developing the craft.

I write email newsletters almost every day. I have several groups who want to hear from me, so I'm duty bound to create content and write.

I wrote this book over three weeks. I wrote my first book over a long weekend. It took me four years to write another. It doesn't matter how long it takes. What does matter is that you propel yourself towards the finish line. And by the finish line, I mean having your book ready to go to print. And you do that word by word.

Some days I can write five or six thousand words. Others, I've struggled to write five or six hundred. For many authors, a few hundred would be a good day.

It's not a competition. There's no league table where you are going to be compared with others for the number of words you write. But I can assure you that *making time* to write is key.

Let me share with you my daily writing secret and how I refined it. I've used this idea for over 20 years and it ensures that I find the time to write every day.

It was October 3rd 1995, I was in New York and due to meet with Harold Evans. Sir Harry, as he became known after his Knighthood, was a publisher - but no ordinary publisher. He was the former editor of the Sunday Times and president and publisher at Random House, one of the biggest publishers in the world. He was the founding editor of Conde Nast Traveller. You could say he was a big cheese in the Big Apple.

I'll always remember that date as it was the day of the OJ Simpson verdict. I'm sure OJ Simpson remembers that day, too. Harold Evans was a busy man. I patiently waited outside his office while his PA offered me coffee and assured me that Mr Evans wouldn't be too much longer. I knew he was very important. His assistant had an assistant.

After a few minutes, his PA asked if I'd like to go into his office. And that's when it happened. As I walked past her desk, she calmly said, 'Mr Heppell, you have 17 minutes.' This had never happened to me before (nor has it since). I'd been given a quarter of an hour, five minutes, half an hour, 10 minutes, or even 'You've got a minute', but never 17.

You truly understand the value of someone's time when their day is broken down by the minute. I've talked about the actual meeting in a couple of my previous books, so I won't replay that now. But I do remember flying home that night and journaling the details of that extraordinary meeting. I wrote: 'His diary was so organised that my meeting was scheduled for 17 minutes and it was just that, to the second.'

Since then, I've used 17 as a technique to get things done.

17 Minute Sprints

Whenever I need to write, but I've procrastinated or I'm finding it challenging, I ask my digital assistant (my iPhone) to give me a 17-minute countdown. Then I start to write.

To find these elusive minutes, stop doing other things that take 17 minutes: Watching the news. Flicking through TikTok or Instagram videos. Binge-watching Netflix or going down YouTube rabbit holes. Instead, just write for 17 minutes. That's all. And if you get past 17 minutes and want to keep going, great, keep going.

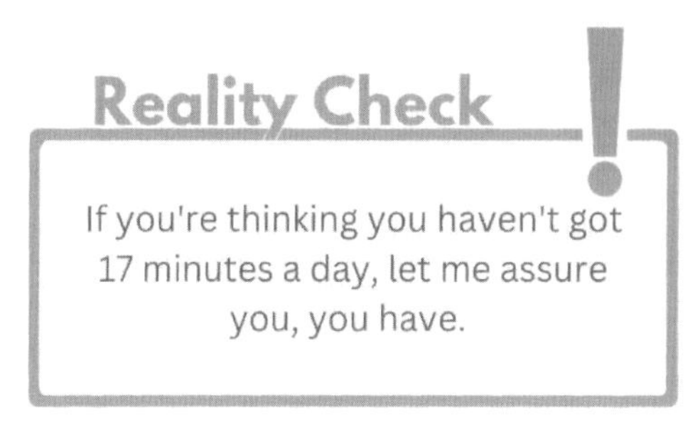

If you're struggling to write for 17 minutes, please just keep at it. See the next chapter on the myth of Writer's Block. 17 Minute Sprints are like a workout at the gym. All the benefit is in the final few repetitions.

I've started to use dictation software for 17 Minute Sprints and it's transformed my writing life. I often use the free software that comes with my computer, but I'm also using something called Otter.ai. This is a clever programme as it sits nicely on my mobile phone; I quickly flick it on and it listens and transcribes everything I say with remarkable accuracy. I can add shortcuts too, so when I say WTB it types, Write That Book. I'm using it now. Cool, eh?

Some people get frustrated with voice transcribing software because it doesn't do what they want it to do straight away. That's like getting frustrated with a two-year-old because they can't do their seven times table. Be patient. It will come. Just test it for 17 minutes at a time and you'll be amazed at how much you can write using voice.

And if you really can't find anything to write, don't worry. It's probably just a case of...

6

Writer's Block

'I'm stuck. I have writer's block. I don't know what to write. Woe is me!'

I don't believe in writer's block and after this chapter, you won't either. If you should ever find yourself in that place where you think you have writer's block, do this instead...

Write Shite

The idea is very simple. When you're staring blankly at a screen and you're wondering where the inspiration is going to come from, I would suggest you don't rely on inspiration, divine intervention, or a bolt of brilliance. Instead, just start to write using the 17-minute sprint idea I've just shared. And just write shite.

You can (and should) aim for 17 minutes of writing shite. When you review your work, I guarantee it's impossible to find a whole 17 minutes of shite. There will be ideas in there that, when you look back, you will discover are good, fantastic or even brilliant.

I would go so far as to say that if you spend 17 minutes writing shite, at least a third of it will be usable, a third may need to be tweaked and a third will need some heavy work on the delete button. That's a bold claim, but I've seen it work many times for many people.

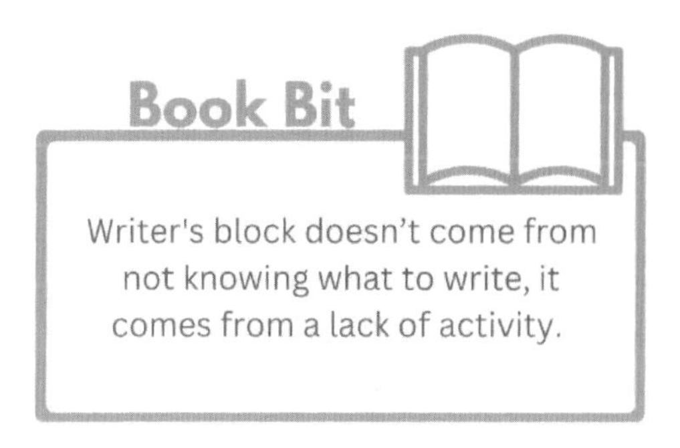

If you don't fancy writing shite, there are some other ways to defeat the dreaded writer's block.

Go backwards to go forwards

Imagine you're driving to a friend's wedding. You follow the directions but with just half an hour before the ceremony, you suddenly realise, horror of horrors, you're lost. What would you do? You could keep driving, desperately looking for a clue.

This may or may not be a good solution; remember the wedding takes place in 30 minutes. You're sure you followed the instructions (btw, this metaphor takes place pre-satnav) you may or may not become even more lost.

Or you could go back a couple of steps.

You recall driving past the White Horse Pub and the White Horse is on the directions. But did you take the second right? Or was it the first right? The best way to find out is to go back to the White Horse and restart your journey from there.

If you're a fiction writer, this could mean going back a chapter to that last decision your main character made. How would things evolve if you gave them a different decision? Go back, test it and see what happens.

If you're writing a children's book and it's lost its pace, think about the last moment when your story had its beat. Now ask, where does the energy want to flow? That's where your story should go.

If it's a memoir, is this mental block because you've lost your pace and things have become a little turgid? Perhaps you could leave this part out and spring forward to something more interesting.

With a non-fiction book, sometimes an idea just isn't strong enough. By going back, you can maybe link it with another idea, as an enhancer rather than a standalone. Go back to the promise to your reader; are you keeping it?

The Library

Another great way to get out of the funk of writer's block is to use the author's secret weapon. The library. Pick up any book from your collection, turn to a random page and just start to read.

It could be an old favourite that might spark new ideas because of the things you like about this book. What can you do to make yours as good? Or it could be something you've never read before. By giving yourself a whack on the side of the head, new ideas start to flow. New information equals new ideas.

I once coached an executive who was looking for the next thing to do with his life. He knew what he was expected to do, but it didn't float his boat. I suggested he go into a newsagent, stand in front of the magazine shelves, close his eyes, move his head around, stop and open his eyes. And then buy whichever magazine he was looking at.

The next day, before he caught a flight, he followed my suggestion to the letter. He visited the newsagents and followed the instructions. When he opened his eyes he was looking directly at a magazine on... fly fishing.

He had no interest in fly fishing, but still he bought the magazine and spent a short flight flicking through it. One of the things he noticed was the passion that anglers had for fishing trips. He also noticed there were few advertisements for accommodation aimed specifically for anglers. An idea started to form. He had an interest in property and after a little research discovered there could be a decent demand for short-term property lets close to popular fishing sites. The following weekend he viewed the first of several rental properties he now owns. His new business idea was born. He now promotes short term lets for fisherman's cottages to anglers and does very well, all because of a random magazine choice.

What might you pick up?

One more idea which is right up there with Write Shite is to...

Talk Shite

Many people, particularly those closest to me, may claim I am an expert at this. However, this isn't about rambling, it's using the power of dictation. Yes, I'm talking about transcription again, but this time it's not for speed – it's for ideas.

One of the things dictation software forces you to do is to keep talking. This creates a stream of consciousness which ends up on your screen/page. Yes, there's a lot of editing needed. However, by forcing the mind to fill space – ie when you're not being interrupted by endless notifications, message pings, the radio, Facebook, tabs open, emails popping up and a dozen other things that demand your attention – it's amazing how your brilliant brain gets on with filling the gap with content.

Old School Idea Generation – Think on Paper

I love this simple idea. Take a blank piece of paper and some coloured pens or pencils. In the centre of the page, write down your issue/challenge.

Then allow your amazing mind to think of four random words. You can use an online 'random word generator', but be careful not to get lost in the rabbit warren of The Google.

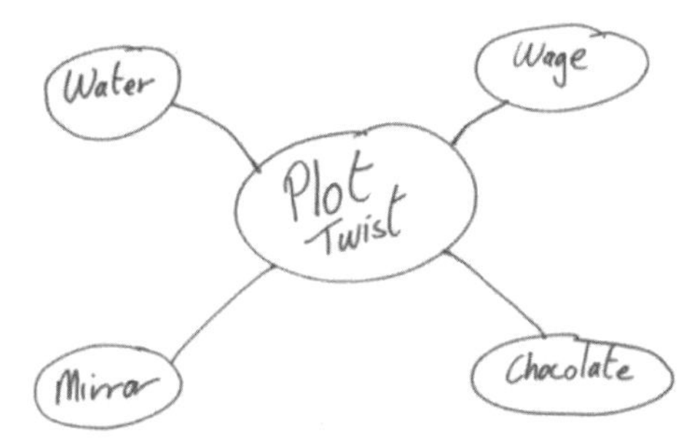

Then use each of those four random words and add four associated words. It should end up looking something like this.

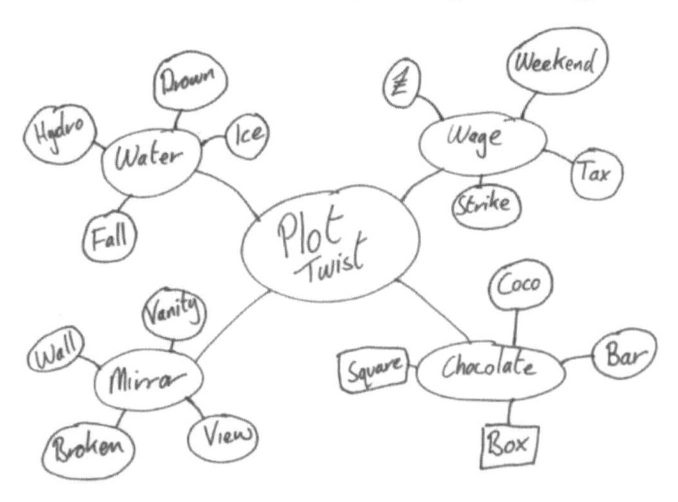

Now look for links. They may not be obvious at first, so allow your imagination to wander across the page. As you find each link, connect it with a different colour.

Make a few notes on what it could mean. Remember, you're not looking for a solution, the next chapter or a big idea, you're simply looking for something to get you over the dreaded writer's block.

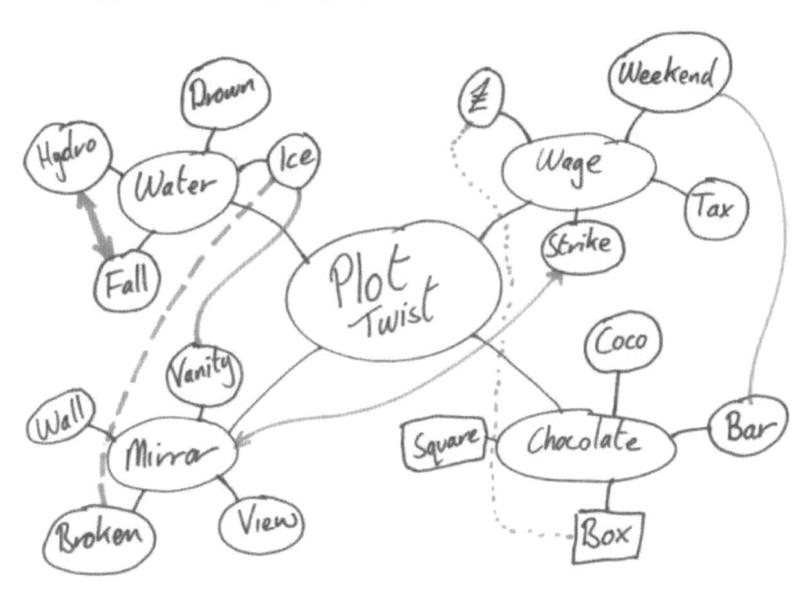

Thinking hard is hard work. Turning those thoughts into words can be harder. Your job as a writer is to do this with consistency. That means, writing for a minimum of 17 minutes every single day. Whether it's writing shite, going back to what you know, taking ideas from other sources, linking random words or filling silence by dictation, one of these will work brilliantly for you.

And all you need is the world to slow down so you can concentrate on...

7

Finding the Time to Write

Starting to write your book is easy, finishing is something else.

The number one reason new writers give for not completing their project is they believe they don't have the time. I get it. I wrote a book on it! Everyone wants to know how to find time.

I believe you can successfully write, publish and sell your book with as little as four or five hours work a week. I'll show you how.

First and foremost, start with changing your mindset around time. Everyone has the same amount. It's how you use it that's key. There are thousands of books (I would recommend '*How to Save an Hour Every Day*') and millions of articles on saving time. But at the end of the day, they are simply tips and tricks. Knowing them means nothing. You must do them.

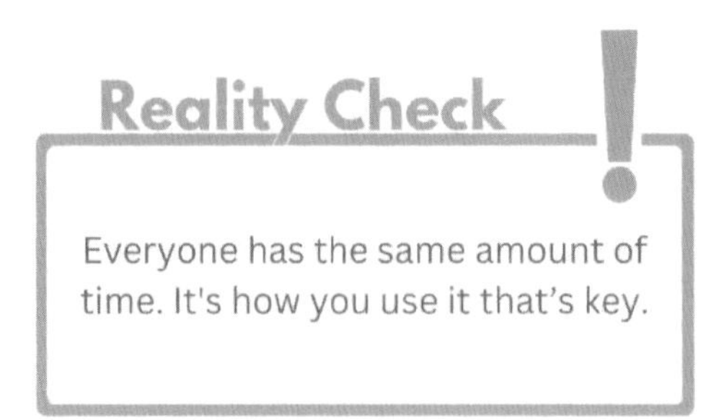

Finding the time to write your book must start with this mindset:

I will find the time to write my book. That means you're going to have to make a few choices.

Here are 10 simple things you can stop and start doing to find the time to write your book:

1. **Don't watch the news**
2. **Cut down on social media**
3. **Cancel your streaming services**
4. **Learn how to say no - nicely**
5. **Get up half an hour earlier or go to bed half an hour later**
6. **Carry a notepad and pen**
7. **Write in sprints. Use the 17-minute sprint idea from Chapter 5**
8. **Learn to use dictation software**
9. **Put 'writing time' in your diary, make an appointment with yourself**
10. **Write in the margins of your life**

Accelerator Weekends

If you're a busy person, schedule some weekends where for two days you focus on writing. But structure them in such a way that you get things done. As part of my Write That Book programme, I organise two Accelerator Weekends. New authors write more in two days than they could in a month and it's mainly down to the structure we use.

Here's what to do:

The pre-start set up

Make sure your family know that you are writing this weekend and you have a place where you won't be disturbed. Day One starts at 10am; that doesn't mean you'll have a lie in, it means you get up, get ready and make sure everything else is done first.

Be Prepared

Have all you need at hand. You start writing at 10am, not setting up your computer or making a cup of tea.

17-Minute Sprints

This is where you write for 17 minutes straight. No let up, breaks to make coffee or downtime. Just write.

3-Minute Mini Break

During these three minutes, you MUST look away from your screen. I use the 20:20:20 method. Every twenty minutes (17 for us) spend twenty seconds looking at least twenty metres into the distance.

Day 1

10:00	17 Minute sprint
10:17	3 Minute mini break
10:20	17 Minute sprint
10:37	3 Minute mini break
10:40	17 Minute sprint
10:57	23 Minute break. Have something to drink, stretch your legs etc.
11:20	17 Minute sprint
11:37	3 Minute mini break
11:40	17 Minute sprint
11:57	3 Minute mini break
12:00	17 Minute sprint
12:17	23 Minute break. Have a cup of something, stretch your legs etc.
12:40	17 Minute sprint
12:57	3 Minute mini break
13.00	17 Minute sprint
13:17	3 Minute mini break
13:20	17 Minute sprint
13:37	Lunch - 23 minutes!
14:00	Repeat the morning
17:17	Review Day 1

Day 2

Repeat Day 1

At the end of your Accelerator Weekend, you will have written for over 10 hours and I promise you will have thousands of lovely words. You can use this method for editing, marketing, tribe building, or anything else on your Write That Book journey.

However, you must start with an intent: If you are supposed to be editing, make sure you edit. If you're supposed to be writing, then write. If you're researching, research.

Avoiding Procrastination

I put the pro in procrastination. If procrastination was an Olympic event, I could represent Great Britain and win gold. Not the next Olympics. I'll do the one after that.

[You've got to love a good procrastination joke. You're even putting off laughing!]

To overcome procrastination, I do these three things.

Schedule

What gets scheduled gets done. When I need to write I put *Writing Time* in my diary.

Most people who want to write a book, but never do, believe they will write when they're not doing other stuff. The reality is writing must be the stuff. Important stuff. So, schedule it.

Do It Now!

Secondly, when I find myself procrastinating, I say these three words out loud three times. Do it now. Do it now! DO IT NOW! Each time I say it louder and by the time I get to the third I'm usually standing and shouting it. This seems to knock my brain into gear and I start. It also terrifies anyone in the vicinity.

Accountability

One of the best ways to be accountable is to set a deadline. Deadlines are brilliant for making you write. As I'm writing this section, I know that this book needs to be launched on a set date next year. I've announced it.

That means my editor has to have copy in a couple of days and if I don't get that copy to her, she will miss the deadline with the designer. And if the designer doesn't get their work done, then the printer can't produce the book. And if the printer can't produce the book I can't sell the book. And I've already taken orders.

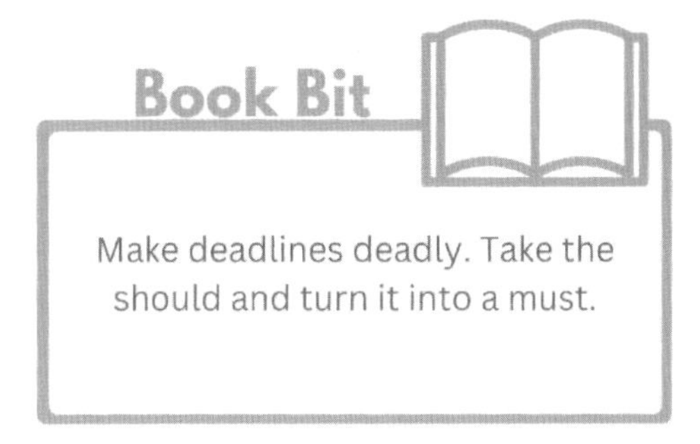

Writing in the margins of your life

If you're unable to arrange Accelerator Weekends or schedule in blocks of writing time for yourself that doesn't mean you won't be able to write your book. You can 'write in the margins of your life'.

I love that phrase. It's not ideal, but you're better off having 10 minutes here and 20 minutes there. One of the best ways to do this is by using dictation software. If you haven't already guessed, yes, I'm a fan.

As the quality of the transcription improves, this method of writing is becoming more and more popular. It's not for everyone but once you know what you want to write and the words are in your head, all you need to do is get them out.

Just talk into the microphone of your computer or phone and have it transcribed. Currently, I'm using Otter.ai. However, I've also used the software that comes with Microsoft Word, Dragon Dictate and also the voice recognition software on my Mac and all of them are pretty good.

Maybe now is a good time to park your writing. Not stop, just park. There are dozens of brilliant books on the art of writing, grammar and prose. I suggest you read any that make you better.

One thing is guaranteed; you won't get it right the first time. That's why you must embrace...

8

Edit That Book

Along with marketing and tribe building, this is the work that most authors dread. The main reason is that editing your book is not as much fun as writing it was, plus you MUST delete some of your work.

Let's take a step back. You don't have to worry about editing something until you've written something. And I would suggest you don't worry about editing until you've written a lot of something.

I once coached a gifted writer who was so crippled with self-doubt that they would write a page, then feel the need to edit the same page before moving on. This practice stifles your flow and nobody wants that.

May I suggest you only start to edit when you've written the first third of your book? Or why not write it all, then edit.

Time to Edit

Like finding the time to write, you need to schedule the time to edit. And you also need to enter into editing with a different mindset.

There are many different types of editing. I think it would be worthwhile giving you a brief overview of each. The first two are:

Editorial Assessment and **Developmental Editing**

This is where an editor will help you to decide on the book as a whole; your idea, concepts, content etc. A good Developmental Editor will make you think hard about your work. If you're writing fiction, they'll drill down on character motivation. If you're writing non-fiction, they'll ask you lots of why and how questions. It's exhausting but you're better off listening and adapting at this stage than having to change huge chunks of your book later.

Author Edit

This first self-edit is where the author goes through their work and tidies everything up. This is where you, as the writer, will spot mistakes, change sentence construction and realise some parts aren't needed and can be cut out - YES CUT OUT! More on this in a moment and other tips to improve the quality of your work.

Copy Editor

This is often mixed up with a proofread. That comes later - but it is similar.

A Copy Editor will work through your whole book, pointing out where you have made grammatical mistakes (often changing them for you at the same time), ensuring that the correct tenses have been used and generally improving the readability of your book. You'll probably argue about the use of the Oxford comma, realise how completely word-blind you have become and thank God they stopped you from looking silly when your book was published.

Proofreader

Contrary to popular belief, a proofread is not at the start of the process. Often writers will say 'I need someone to proofread this'. What they mean is they need someone to *Copy Edit* this.

Proofreading comes at the end when you receive your sample copy of your typeset book. Proofreading is checking to make sure that the words are on the right pages, that your wonderful designer/typesetter hasn't duplicated anything and that something hasn't gone awry during the publishing process.

There are many types of editors and, in most cases, you'll be doing all of these editing jobs yourself. Let me clarify.

Imagine you've written 5,000 words - well done. I suggest you put those 5,000 words through an online grammar checker. Microsoft Word can do this (most word processing programmes can) but there are also some clever online ways to check. I use Grammarly and Hemingway.

Grammarly spots silly mistakes; like using the same word twice, missing commas, and of course, dodgy spellings. Hemingway checks readability and will offer suggestions on sentences that are too long, read difficulty and other clever bits.

Once you've run your copy through these programmes, the next stage is to make your work read better.

Read Out Loud

If there is one tip which I know will make a massive difference to the quality of writing, it's reading your work out loud.

I know this can be embarrassing, so set aside some time, find somewhere private, have your work ready and promise me you will read it out loud. This isn't mumbling out loud, it's reading; reading as if you were at a Book Festival and you've been asked as a special guest to share a chapter. Project!

You will spot complicated sentences, words that don't make sense and even times when you're just plain boring. As you get to the end of each paragraph, go back, make your adjustments and then read it out loud again. I know this is hard work but this one technique will improve the quality of your book more than any other.

Cut, cut, cut!

'If in doubt, take it out', is another of my mantras. If there's any part of your book that you know shouldn't be there or you're unsure about, either rewrite it or take it out.

Just because you've written the words doesn't mean that your book must include them. Every word needs to earn its place.

From the first draft to the final print, I can take out a third of what I've written. I don't always delete. If I take large sections out, I add them to another file, then later I can create bonus material, add to the audio version or use it for newsletters. Words are never wasted.

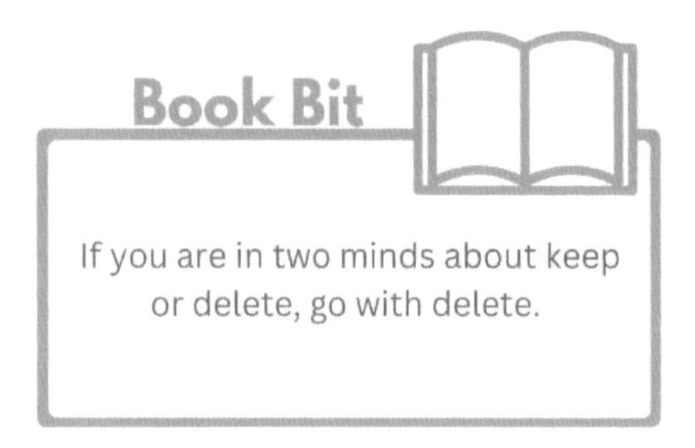

Editing like this is particularly important with children's books. Some first-time children's authors believe that because there are fewer words, it's easier to write. The opposite is true. Every single word must land. There is no space for wasted words.

Another type of book, for which a good edit is crucial, is an autobiography.

Most autobiographies are too long. This is because the author is writing on a subject they know EVERYTHING about. And without a development editor, the author thinks the reader needs to know everything too.

Legal

One of the most common questions I've been asked as an author coach, especially by people who are writing autobiographies, is whether they should or could name people, use quotes, brand names, etc. I even had one person who wanted to use the famous Harry Potter phrases to title each chapter!

I'd suggest you remove all risks. Even if you change somebody's name, but they can be recognised by your words, you're still at risk of being sued for defamation.

Remember: If in doubt, leave it out.

Chapter Layout

It's worthwhile thinking about how your words will look on a page. The days of long chapters, paragraphs with hundreds of words and a narrative where the reader needs a spreadsheet to work out who's saying what and when, are over. These days, most readers want shorter chapters, shorter paragraphs and very clear direction.

The editing process shouldn't be rushed. Often authors get off to a good start, then they become bored with editing, they understandably just want to get it done and rush the second half of their book. It shows.

Take some time, do it properly and Edit That Book.

My Caveat

I do not doubt that this book will contain errors. All books do. If you spot one, let me know. One of the wonderful things about publishing today is how simple it is to change your manuscript in future editions, with little or no cost.

And don't fret about mistakes. In my book ***17***, there's a mistake on the first page. So far, only two people have spotted it (and have let me know). Don't beat yourself up too much if things aren't perfect the first time around. It's more important that you write, publish and sell your slightly flawed book than to have a perfect book that never goes to print.

10 tips to help you edit

1. **Schedule Edit Time.** What gets scheduled gets done
2. **Gamify.** Reward yourself with a treat for every major mistake you uncover and every 100 unnecessary words you lose. I love this Flip It thinking as, by rewarding yourself, you're positively looking for what's wrong rather than trying to avoid it
3. **Read Out Loud.** If there's only one piece of advice you take from me to help with your edit, it has to be reading out loud
4. **Use Software.** Technology is amazing and programmes such as Grammarly and Hemingway will help
5. **Take breaks.** It's easy to go word-blind when you don't take breaks
6. **Don't Cheat.** As soon as you start thinking to yourself, 'That'll do', then it's time to stop. This is where a good edit quickly becomes a poor edit

7 **Use Beta Readers.** After you've completed your first pass, give your chapters to others and ask them to find some silly mistakes. There's an essay on using beta readers in Chapter 23

8 **If in doubt, leave it out**

9 **Is this interesting?** If you're bored reading your work, your prospective reader has already switched off

10 **Pay someone to do it for you**

When to Stop Editing

Sooner or later you'll have to stop editing and push the publish button. Your book will never be perfect, there will always be a tweak here or an edit there to make it (in your mind) that bit better. But publish you must and that means deciding when enough is enough as it's time to...

Sell That Book

On the front cover of this book is a promise. You will write, publish and ***sell*** your book.

There are thousands of books on how to write and dozens of books on how to publish, but very few on how to sell. That's why many authors only ever write one book, because of the crushing disappointment when they only sell a handful of copies.

This is especially true when new writers pay a small fortune to have their book 'professionally produced', thinking (naively) that once it's out there, people will buy it.

Whether you're published with Penguin or going straight to Kindle, it's up to you to sell your book.

9

Who'll Buy My Book?

Introducing your Avatar.

Imagine an upside-down pyramid; that's the UK population (I know this book is being read all over the world but I know the number here). 66 million people - it's a huge funnel, so, let's narrow it down:

Take the people who read books and you could safely half it. And take the people who have bought one book or more in the last year (40%).

Next, cut it again for the people who would read your genre.

Chop that in half. Now, it's people who would buy your type of book.

Another slice and you have potential readers who know you.

One more final chop and you have those who know, like and trust you and would be happy to buy your book.

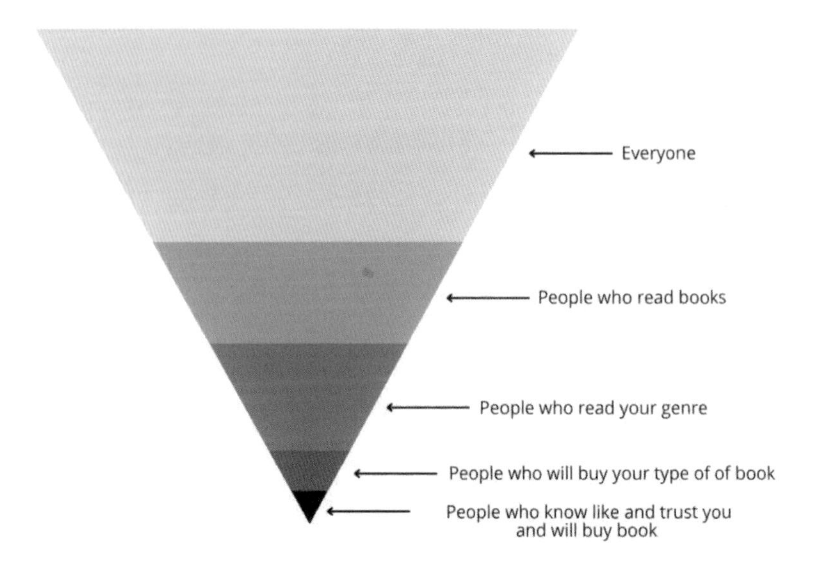

From sixty million, you're down to thousands. And that's okay. Because when we flip this triangle, it changes from being a funnel to a pyramid. And all you're going to do is focus on the top of the pyramid, the star on the Christmas Tree, the tip of the peak. You get the idea.

80% of your time is going to be focused on that top point
15% on the next block
And maybe 5% on the next

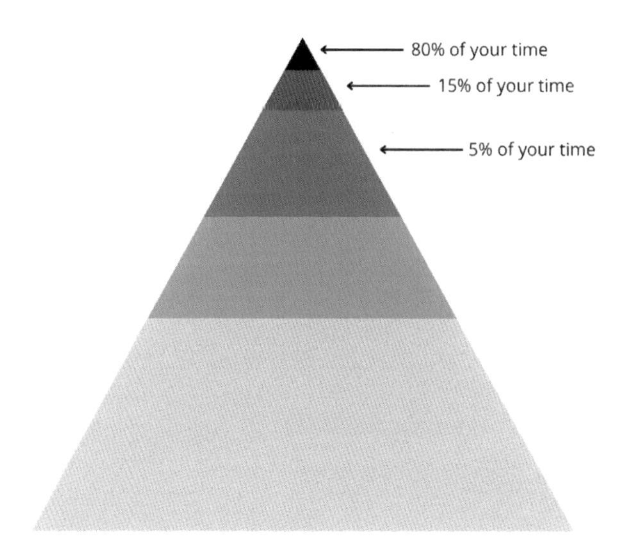

This wonderful 80% of your focus group of people are known as your Avatars. People who know, like and trust you, will be interested in your book and happy to buy it.

Just for fun, why not describe your Avatar?

> 'Meet Betty, she's 58, married with two grown up kids, lives in Yorkshire, works in People & Culture and loves to bake. She likes nothing more than snuggling up in front of the fire with a good crime thriller. Detective books are her favourite. She doesn't watch much TV but if she does, she's drawn to Vera or Poirot. She has a cat called Mr Snaggles and her husband is Terry.'

From this moment, your marketing plan is to focus on targeting readers like Betty. Here's how...

10

Build Your Tribe

In my Write That Book Masterclass, the number one regret that almost every published author has, is that they wish they had started Tribe-building earlier. Waiting until your book has been published, or is close to being published and then starting to build a Tribe is a sure-fire way to frustration. Worse than that, you can come across as desperate when suddenly, out of nowhere, you're trying to get people to buy your book which is launched next week.

Tribe Building isn't marketing. Marketing is broadcasting you as an author brand and the availability of your book. You'll see some smart ways to do this in Chapter 12. Tribe Building is all about connections.

You may be thinking, why should I bother; I just want to sell my book to my friends, family and randoms I meet on trains. Here's why. First, you'll be amazed at how many of your friends and family won't want to buy your book (you may do better with randoms on trains). This can be crushing. Some years ago, while I was arranging a book blast, I messaged my brother asking if he would buy my book on Amazon at a set time. He messaged me back saying he wouldn't be buying my book. It was only £9.99. I was devastated.

In reality, it was my fault. He had no vested interest in the book. I hadn't talked to him about it. I hadn't told him I was writing it. And then suddenly I was asking him to buy it. Why should he?

Your Tribe is an extension of your friendship group. And the more friends you have, the more people there are who are *likely* (not certain) to buy your book.

Remember your Avatar - Betty? That's the person who is most likely to want to buy your book. These 'Betty's' have 'hang-outs'. Places they go where they are happy to talk about your subject all day. And these hangouts are most likely to be online, which means you can access them. There are Facebook groups, Instagram hashtags, LinkedIn groups, TikTok themes, Twitter communities and whatever the next social media concept might be. There are groups for everything. Your job is to connect with those communities to build your Tribe.

And here's how you do it.

Don't go into these worlds announcing you're a writer with a book coming out. Not just yet. Maybe have 'Author' in your profile description. You may get people asking about it and that's good, but don't shout about it.

Tribe Party

Think about Tribe Building as going to a party where you only know a couple of other guests. Let's say you're writing a book about a manhunt which takes place after a murder in a castle. It's set in the 1970's around a mining community in North Wales. At the party, your mutual friend introduces you to Askar and Fredrick. Askar is an analyst, originally from Kent (Askar isn't their real name, it's their earth name). They like nothing more than waking early and completing their daily 90-minute yoga session, followed by meditation and a chia seed latte. Most evenings, Freddie prepares a macrobiotic meal which they enjoy with a glass of fermented grapefruit juice. After a couple of minutes, you find you're glazing over and stifling a yawn. You have nothing in common with Askar and Freddie.

A couple of minutes later, you're introduced to Gwyneth and Tam. Tam comes from a family of miners and Gwyneth grew up in North Wales. They're members of a local history society and frequently visit castles. They both love to read and Gwyneth likes nothing more than a good murder mystery.

No, not yet! Wait... Wait...

You remember reading, *If you want to be interesting, be interested.* So, you ask them questions, find out more and quickly confirm that these people will be perfect readers of your book.

However, you continue to bite your tongue and hold back from announcing that you're writing a book.

You wait, because sooner or later they're going to ask you what you do. And it's at that point you can say, 'Well, you'll never believe it, but I'm writing a book set in North Wales. It's a murder mystery, that takes place in a mining community in the 1970's.

What will Gwyneth and Tam say next? 'Oh, that's nice.' or 'Wow, how do we buy a copy?'

You can then ask them for their details and ask for permission to add them to your list.

Or if you're really smart, you'll take out your mobile phone, open up your website's signup page (see Marketing) and ask them to pop their details in straightaway. That way you have the perfect opt-in.

Then you stay in touch with Gwyneth and Tam and let them know when you are going to be publishing. Maybe you send them some information about the book, the first chapter or a photograph of you at the castle working hard doing your research. Anything that will maintain their interest until you are ready to take an order.

You also need to find out where they 'hang-out' online.

Is there a Local History Society Facebook group you could join? If so, go for it. But when you join, do exactly the same as you've done at the party.

Show interest first, find out about others and be interested in them. Then eventually, you can start to promote what you do. You'll know when to do this; it's when they start to ask about you.

I call this, 'Putting deposits in the emotional bank account'. I believe you need to have at least six deposits in someone's emotional bank account before you can take one withdrawal.

And the withdrawal, on this occasion, is 'Will you buy my book?'

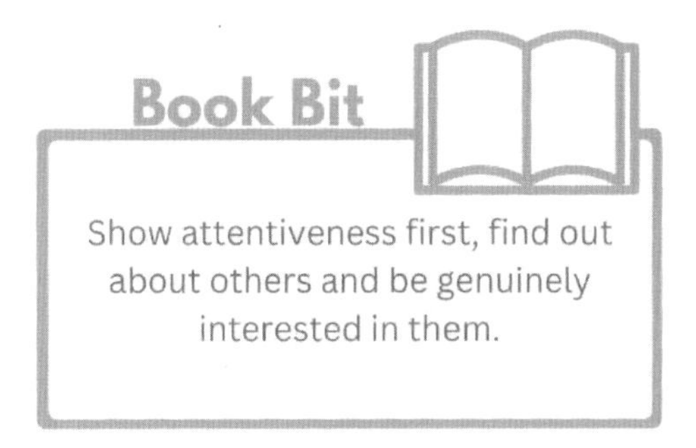

The party and online interactions are the same thing. Don't join Askar's chia latte drinking yoga group if you want to sell a murder mystery set in North Wales.

Do join the Local History Society, the Anglesey Appreciation Society or Creepy Castles of Wales, because that's where you're most likely to find the people who are going to be interested in your book.

Facebook Pages & Groups

Once you start to build these relationships, people will begin to ask what you do and want a method to connect with you. A Facebook Page or Group is a great way to do this. It's free and you know how much I love free. And it's familiar; most people know how to use Facebook. If you're not happy with Facebook, there are other social media channels you can use from Twitter to TikTok, LinkedIn to Instagram.

Choose one or two of the channels that you're going to use to connect, talk about yourself and your work and post regularly. I mainly use Facebook as it fits well with my Avatar. I rarely say 'Buy a book'. Instead, I create interest in my books via stealth.

I might post a simple question. Often it doesn't have to have anything to do with my work. And it's usually these ones that have had the best responses.

When I first set up my *How to Be Brilliant* Facebook Group, I tried to make everything about *How to Be Brilliant* the book, the keynote and the coaching. I would ask questions and create and share posts that were linked to the core messaging of *How to Be Brilliant*. I had mixed results.

One day I was working with a coaching client - the owner of a ladies clothing store - who had an amazing social media following, particularly on Facebook. She offered me this pearl of wisdom:

'Michael, you're asking questions that are too hard for people to answer. You're making people think and on Facebook people don't have time to think. Just keep it simple.'

I asked for her advice and this is what she suggested: 'Post a picture of lots of different biscuits and just ask, What's your favourite biscuit*?'

At this time, I was averaging maybe five or six comments on a good post. So I followed her advice and I posted; 'What's your favourite biscuit?' And within two days I had over 100 comments. A couple of weeks later I'd surpassed 300!

It's an easy question. Everyone has an answer. It's people talking about their favourite subject - themselves (not biscuits!). There were even some arguments! Bourbon versus custard cream was particularly vicious. Somebody even started a thread about whether 'to dunk or not to dunk'.

You may be wondering what this has got to do with writing a book and building a Tribe. Me too, but then I discovered the magic of engagement. This is about Facebook users seeing (or more likely Facebook showing) Michael Heppell and *How to Be Brilliant* rather than another video of a kid sticking a tube of Mentos in a bottle of Coke. The more followers who comment, the more followers who are shown the post. They are connecting, answering questions and you are building a community. A Tribe!

Now you have their interest, it's time to...

*Mine is a Hobnob - it cannot be beaten.

11

Involve Your Tribe

Once you have your book ready to launch, keep going with asking questions - but now make the questions about your book. Three that work well for authors are:

Help me pick a cover

Have two versions of your book cover and ask people which is their favourite. You will get loads of comments. Plus, a lot of people who don't even realise you're writing a book will start asking questions like: 'When is your book being published?', 'Can you tell me more?' You can then direct those people to your sales page.

Character names

If you're writing a fiction book, it's wonderful to ask for advice on a character's name. You can use polls to do this, eg I have an evil character in my book; which of these names do you think sounds most scary? A) Mickey McManus B) Mike Killsalot C) Max Purple.

Ask a question

Should I kill my hero?

Do you think business books should contain real-life examples?

At what age do children start independently reading?

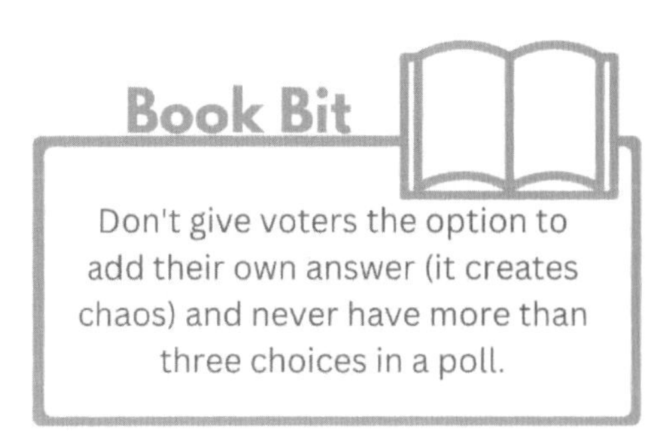

Make things simple to encourage comments, then respond to every comment. This is hard work. However, if you take the time to comment on what your tribe have added to your group or page, it's a huge deposit in their emotional bank accounts. By responding to their comment, you give a follower a moment of significance. Yes, the person who owns this page or group has taken the time to respond to my comment. And it needs to be more than just 'Great', 'Wow' or 'Thank you'. But it doesn't have to be too much. One or two sentences are all it takes.

Remember, you're going to need a minimum of five or six deposits in the emotional bank account for every withdrawal, especially in the early days.

Consistency is key

Initially, you will be doing this work for zero payback. You'll wonder whether my advice is completely duff and if you're wasting your time. That's when you must keep going. Sooner or later there's a tipping point, you'll crack the algorithm and you'll become more visible to more people. People who you don't know you - potential new Tribe members.

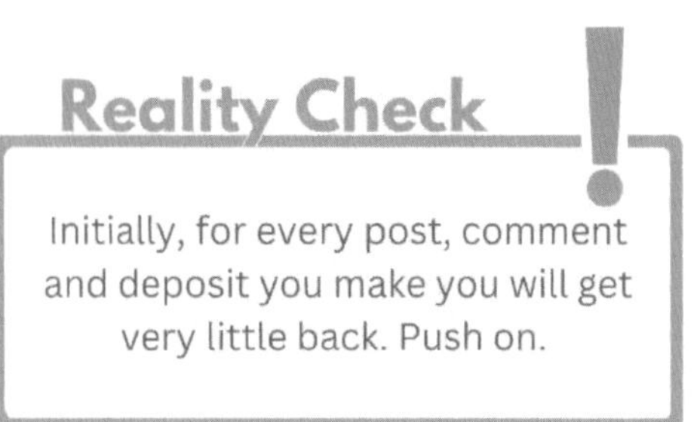

All social media companies reward people who create content and comment on other posts. It's their way of maintaining interest, but it's not consistent. You will get some boosts (hooray!) then things will go flat (booo), then you get some more boosts (hooray!) and then guess what? Yep, things will go flat again.

Keep going, keep on keeping on. Test and measure what works and you'll soon understand what your Tribe does and doesn't like. What may turn them on and what may turn them off. It might not be what you think.

To sell books you need to become a marketeer. You won't have a big budget, so it's best to learn...

12

Marketing for free
(or at least for buttons)

There are lots of ways you can market your book and it shouldn't be too expensive. In fact, many magical marketing methods are free - stealth marketing.

Open your mind to these simple, yet effective, ideas. Choose your favourites and test them. You must get out of your comfort zone a little - it will be worth it.

Podcasts

I don't think it's a good idea to start your own podcast; unless you're prepared to do the work of creating and recording regular content, sharing it via multiple platforms and marketing your podcast alongside marketing your book.

However, the huge growth in podcasts means podcasters are looking for guests. Here's where you come in. Being a guest on a podcast is an easy way to promote your book.

If you are going to be a guest on a podcast, there are a few things you can do to make sure you present yourself well. Then listeners will like, be interested and want to find out more about you and ultimately buy your book.

Signature Stories

Make sure you have a few *signature stories* rehearsed and ready to share. These are short stories you can effortlessly recount. They only last for one or two minutes, always get a good response and make the podcaster feel like you have shared something very special with them and their audience.

Because it's a signature story, you will tell it hundreds of times. You might tire of it but that doesn't matter, as the podcaster's audience is hearing it for the first time.

I have four or five signature stories which I use to promote various books.

For example, if I'm a podcast guest talking about my book, ***The Edge** how the best get better*, I share the same story about how I did my research.

It involves me interviewing two very different 'Edgers'. The former Head of the British Army, General Sir Mike Jackson and one of the world's greatest restaurateurs, Danny Meyer. I interviewed Sir Mike one day and Danny the next. On comparing the notes I'd taken, I found many of their answers were very similar. It turns out that Edgers may have different roles, but their methodology often remains the same.

I finish with, 'It looked like General Sir Mike Jackson could be a great restaurateur and Danny Mayer could run the British army.'

It's a good story in that it has a natural flow between the start, middle and end. As well as creating some interest, it also demonstrates I've done my research and yes I manage to do a bit of name-dropping in the story too. Name-dropping is acceptable when you're promoting your work.

Some practical thoughts on being a podcast guest

If you're going to be a podcast guest, make it easy for the podcaster to work with you. Simple things like how to connect with you. Contact details, telephone number etc.

Make them the star. Podcasters are not hospital radio DJ's; they have egos that need to be fed. Big them up! Having said that, I've met some hospital radio DJ's with huge egos!

Give value first. You'll get the chance to promote your book, but no one cares about you as a guest until they feel like they know *you* first.

Invest in a half-decent microphone, wear headphones and smile when you speak.

ALWAYS promote the podcasts you have appeared on on your own social media channels. Thank the host and direct your followers to the podcast.

Keep it short.

Radio

Local radio stations are always looking for quality guests. And somebody from the local area who is writing, or has just published their book, is an interesting guest. Don't you agree?

It's one of the easiest ways to promote to a wider market, so long as you're prepared to do a little work first.

In the main, this involves picking up the phone and asking for the producer of show X. Don't be shy, tell them what you're doing and what you can offer.

Make sure you've done your research and you know which shows have regular guests, search The Google for the name of the show's producer (producers and researchers are better to make contact with than presenters, it's their job to find guests) and go directly to them.

Even if they aren't looking for someone like you at that point, offer to send your details and say you would be happy to be a guest at any time.

As a rule of thumb, breakfast shows may have more guests, but they do tend to be on the air for a shorter time period. Afternoon shows have fewer guests (and listeners), but you can grab more airtime.

When you're a guest on a local radio show, unless asked, you must leave it to the presenter to promote your book. They will normally do this for you at the end of the interview. If you go on air and start by saying, 'My book's available on Amazon, here it is, it's only £9.99, all you have to do is go to my website, it's www.VickyTheAuthor.com... etc', you can be pretty certain that the normally placid presenter will be thinking and planning how to quickly get rid of you.

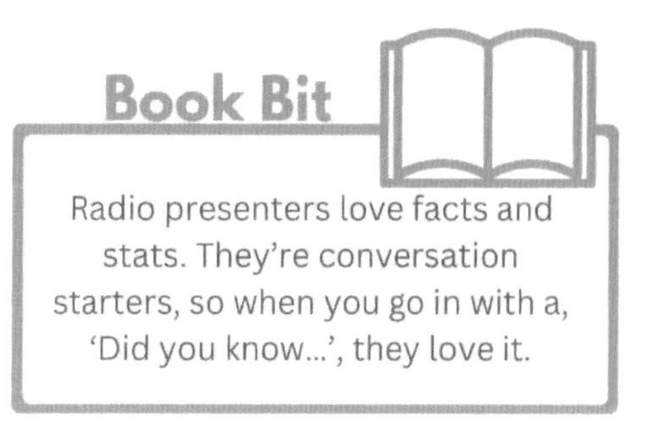

Be an interesting interviewee who's able to share why you've written your book. Recount your signature stories and detail what the reader will gain from your work, then the presenter will be more likely to promote your book.

Reality Check !

Do not expect the tills to ring immediately after a radio appearance unless you are lucky enough to be featured on a national station.

Marketing like this works because you create multiple touch points to build your 'author brand'. Mix your radio appearance with; a piece in the local paper, a Facebook mention and some chat between friends and you'll continually build your profile. Marketing experts love this 'omnipresent' type of promotion. This is where people see and hear you several times via different mediums and when they see your name, that builds familiarity.

Fingers crossed that familiarity draws them towards you and buying your book.

Bookshops

Local bookshops are seeing a rise in popularity but are still fighting for existence. If you can, make friends with your local bookshop and give them great reasons to stock your book. This includes being a good customer and buying your favourite books from them, mentioning them on your social media channels, podcasts or radio interviews you're invited on and ultimately, letting them have a fair percentage of the profit on the sale of your book (at least 40%).

Do this and you may find they will be happy to feature you as a local author.

You could offer to do a talk in the shop and promote this to your Tribe.

When Roger Wilson-Crane wrote his book Certified, much of it was set in the Yorkshire Dales. He contacted a local bookshop, Limestone Books in Settle, and not only did they stock the book, but they also gave it a table display.

Marketing on Amazon

Many new authors think that once their book is on Amazon, as if by magic, readers will find it.

Think about it like this. Imagine Amazon is a physical bookshop. It's the size of a football pitch, their bookshelves are six high and they stock just one copy of each book.

Now consider that's just floor one and this Amazon bookshop has 30 floors. Millions and millions of books across thousands of shelves.

And your book is on the ninth floor, row 36, on the fifth shelf, 132 books from the right.

The chances of somebody walking through the door and finding your book are, at best, remote. That's why bookshops, including the behemoth Amazon, break down their books into sections.

This clever system was created in 1876 by the chief librarian at Columbia University, Melville Dewey. His brain was melting, trying to locate books, so he created the Dewey Decimal Classification as a way to organise. His original 10 main classifications started as a pamphlet and is now a thick book with thousands of classifications and sub-classifications. He was definitely a clever chap, although unfortunately a racist and sexual predator, too. Interesting what you're remembered and categorised for.

Amazon and friends have gone even further with their classifications. Online books now carry detailed 'metadata', which is where you can select a series of keywords to describe your book. If you were writing a book about witches who lived in a lighthouse, set in Cornwall during the late 1800's, then you can add this information to your metadata while posting your book.

This is still marketing. It's still marketing because focusing on the right metadata helps that clever algorithm to make it easier for your reader to find you. It's worthwhile searching The Google for videos (some produced by Amazon) on metadata and how to boost your book. Take some time to think about your book, the information and the classifications that go with it.

I could spend the next 20 pages describing to you in great detail how to do this, but the chances are that by the time I'm done, the information will be out of date. Just ask The Google and you'll quickly find out how to add this valuable marketing information to your book

Social Media

Here's another common misconception. If you share 'content' on social media, people will immediately see your posts and think wow, I must buy that book.

Guess what? Yep, there's a little more to it than that. I write a lot about Tribe Building and I'll mention it again and again. Social Media is where Marketing and Tribe Building overlap and it's where you need to be consistent, interesting and entertaining if you want to be noticed.

What you say and share needs to be consistent with your core beliefs, that's why you need an...

13

Author Brand

Are you clear on your author brand?

The first thing I would suggest you do is to understand and be crystal clear about your author brand. This starts with your *Brand Essence*. Grant Marshall, Creative Director with the brilliant digital consultancy DECIDE. advises authors to answer these questions to discover their brand essence.

Credibility

Why should people believe in you?

Functionality

What do you fundamentally do?

Competitive Differentiators

What sets you apart from the rest of the market?

Personality

What characterises the way you look, talk and behave?

There are no right or wrong answers to these questions and you don't have to be in the top 1% in any of these areas. It's more the combination of these four key areas that make you unique.

Once you have clearly defined what type of author you are it's your core, your essence, your authentic self. Then it's much easier to share stories, posts and information about you and your book which fits with your author brand.

For example, if you're writing a book about cats and the primary reason you're doing this is that you are fanatical about our furry friends, that needs to translate to your author brand.

You could be writing a fictional book about cats or a book about how to take care of adopted cats. This doesn't matter. What's important is that your author brand authentically represents who you are.

Write That Book Masterclass member, Jennifer Flint, wrote a brilliant book called *Wild Egg. The story of one woman's search for her child-free life*.

Jennifer is passionate about helping other women to understand, make informed decisions about and come to terms with whatever they decide about having children, or not. It's an area that I knew little about, but Jennifer is so passionate that you cannot help but connect with her and her author brand. When *Wild Egg* was published, many people already knew what she stood for. She was asked to appear in and on different media outlets; print, radio and even TV to talk about why she wrote her book. This is great author marketing and starts with the foundation of your author brand.

There are dozens of other marketing ideas sprinkled around this book. Some will work all of the time, all will work some of the time. What's important is that you test the marketing ideas and see what works best for you.

Here are 10 ways to successfully use social media to market your author brand:

1 Post Great Content

It sounds obvious but sometimes authors post rubbish and wonder why they don't get comments or likes. It's worthwhile spending a little time deep-thinking about the message you want to give and who it's aimed at. Then create some great content to accompany that.

In the next chapter, I will turn this on its head.

2 Use Images

But don't steal pictures. Use photographs you've taken or use sites which allow you to repost. If it's true that a picture is worth 1,000 words, then every post should have a picture.

3 Go Live

Social media loves it when people present live videos. It doesn't have to be long, just a few minutes of sharing, or an insight into whatever you're up to. You'll quickly find that more people react to those videos, many more than to a pre-recorded video or static image.

4 Create Video

If you post a video - and you can - add subtitles. 69% of users switch their volume off in a public place (how I wish it were more!) and an amazing 25% who watch videos online, watch them all without sound. If you have subtitles, people watch for longer.

5 Ask Questions

Give people a reason to interact with your post.

5.5 Answer Questions

Respond to the responses.

6 Re-share

Repost other people's content. It's flattering for the person who is being re-shared and it saves you from constantly creating new content. Sharing content, helping and supporting other authors/people who have similar values is a cool thing to do.

7 Be Current

If there's something topical happening, create a post about it. Search for which special day it might be. There's a day for everything - from obvious seasonal events to obscure celebrations. Look up National Day and add a date. Be prepared for the brilliantly bonkers.

8 Be Consistent

This is one of the most difficult, yet most important things, that you can do when you're posting on social media. If you sporadically post two or three times, then wait for a couple of weeks and then do a couple more, that's ok. But it's not as powerful as doing two posts each week. Remember, not everyone's going to see your content. So you can post as many times as you like.

9 Use a Scheduler

These are online programmes where you can create your content once and post it on several social media sites. You can also schedule it to post in advance, sometimes weeks ahead. This means you can create a load of content one morning, schedule it and it will post automatically. But be careful; sometimes people use this system, then forget what they've scheduled, the news changes and suddenly something inappropriate is published.

10 Keep Going

This isn't about immediate gratification. Yes, it's nice to get 'likes' and comments. But even if you don't; keep posting, keep sharing and keep putting out quality content. It will pay off in the end.

At this point, you could be feeling overwhelmed. It's worth taking a moment to consider that you don't have to do all of this, all at once. There are some possible shortcuts and accelerators. One is knowing how to...

14

PR That Book

When I wrote my book, *How To Save an Hour Every Day* I knew it would be successful.

The promise is in the title, but I wanted to add something a little more exciting and I did it with one word. And that word was - *Guaranteed.* I came up with a PR stunt that was intrinsically linked with the book, deciding and promoting that my promise would be backed up by a 100% total satisfaction guarantee. Put simply, if you buy this book, use the ideas and you don't save an hour every day we will give you your money back.

This quickly became 'I will give you your money back', as my publisher was terrified by the idea of having to refund dissatisfied readers. For me, it was a no-brainer. All I had to do was make sure enough people bought the book and liked it.

How to Save an Hour Every Day was published in April 2011, by Pearson, one of the biggest publishers in the world. I still love them and I'm grateful for the opportunity they gave me, especially in my early days as a writer. However, I had a couple of meetings with the marketing department and quickly realised that the only way this book was going to get anything like the publicity it deserved, was if I marketed it and created a PR programme myself.

A word of warning: You can learn a lot from other writer's success stories, but you can learn a lot from their failures too. This was mine.

To promote *Save an Hour*, we found, and paid, a PR agency that loved the idea (dahhling) and promised national publicity for the book. This was in exchange for a mere... I still can't bring myself to write the amount, but let's just say, that number you just thought of - it was more. Eyewatering.

When the book was launched, the PR machine was well and truly on a roll. There were a couple of great opportunities, including a double-page spread in the Mail on Sunday plus the possibility of national radio and television interviews.

Of course, sod's law kicked in. A major news story broke on the Friday before the Mail piece which meant that my '10 Ways to Save an Hour Every Day' double-page feature ended up being bumped from print to online.

But the most embarrassing was the television debut. Readers from the UK will know the name Alan Titchmarsh. Alan became famous for his gardening programmes, his gentle cashmere jumper-wearing personality and his comforting appeal to a woman of a particular age. You can fill in the gaps.

Knowing this, ITV gave him his very own chat show and I was booked to appear as a guest, specifically to promote *How To Save an Hour Every Day.*

Here's the challenge. *The Alan Titchmarsh Show* was televised at 3pm on weekday afternoons. Who do you think the audience might have been? Busy people, who don't seem to have enough hours in the day? Those who are desperate to find any technique that will help them gain valuable moments to spend on the more important things in life? Something to help them find time to be with their kids, exercise or land that next big deal? Folk looking for a business strategy and format rather than existing in a frantic day-to-day grind?

Or predominantly retired women, who enjoy nothing more than spending a cosy afternoon with Alan, while sitting on the sofa with a nice cup of tea?

I had a book with a promise to give busy people time and I was talking to an audience who only had time. I think my piece was sandwiched somewhere between a debate on heating allowance and an outside broadcast from an ostrich farm in Kent.

We did sell some extra copies. Maybe it was grandmothers who were worried about their twenty-something grandchildren not having the time to visit, but nowhere near enough traction to bring a return on our investment.

Then I discovered how to really market my books and the clue is in that last story, but it has nothing to do with ostriches.

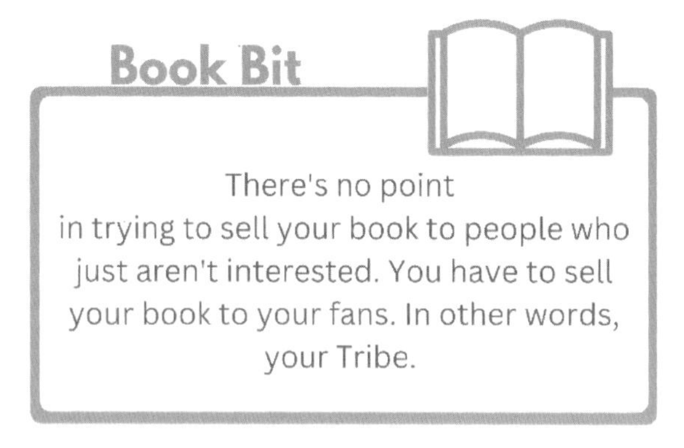

Your Tribe is anyone who will be prepared to spend money on your work because they **already have a connection** with you.

And this works for every genre. Whether you're writing a children's book or a scientific journal, you must build a Tribe. And one of the best times to connect with your Tribe is when you...

15

Launch That Book

There's an amazing way for any author to make an impact, raise their profile and sell lots of books. It's called a book launch and they are brilliant. But only if you organise and host a book launch properly. In this chapter, I'm going to cover three different types of book launches. Online launches, physical (in-venue) launches and hijack launches.

But let's start by convincing you why you should have a book launch. First, having a date for a book launch will focus your mind. The last thing you want as an author is to set a date for a book launch and then not have a book to sell.

Having a launch date is a great way to motivate you, not just to write that book but to publish that book and then sell that book.

Next, a book launch is not just a celebration; it's an opportunity for some great publicity.

And finally, and most importantly, to boost sales.

Since I created Write That Book, I've attended lots of book launches. So far, I've seen mixed results. From the Zoom meeting with six friends where they all had a nice chat but didn't sell any books, to 100-person theatre events where the audience left with multiple copies as 'the ultimate gift for friends and family'.

You always remember your first book launch. Mine was for *How to Be Brilliant* and I was terrified. Who was I to even call myself an author, never mind organise an event to launch my book.

Would anyone be interested? Would anyone want to come?

I needn't have worried, people love to be invited to book launches, there's something about them that feels quite sophisticated and they're a little different from the usual boring networking events. Of course, launching a book called *How to Be Brilliant* I had to have a brilliant book launch. We had themed cocktails, my publisher came to talk about why she thought *How to Be Brilliant* was her most exciting launch of the year (she probably said that to all her authors) and we had 200 guests who could all afford to buy books. Whether they would was a different question.

We had a fun host who gave a short warm-up and then introduced my publisher, Rachael Stock. Rachael talked about her company, Pearson, and how they had the opportunity to select, from hundreds of writers, just a handful of authors they wanted to publish. And how excited she was to be able to work with me. My heart soared, my head swelled and my Mum (naturally in the front row) spontaneously combusted.

Then it was my turn. I talked about why I'd written the book and the content readers would enjoy. But I also remembered to add a piece at the end about the **F.A.B**. That's the features, advantages and benefits of the book. Just listing the contents is a feature. Sharing what someone would get from those contents is an advantage. How they might use that advantage to be a better person, be happier, more competent and successful in any area of their life is the real benefit. Luckily, I remembered to share those key, important points. When you launch your book, you should too.

Then I asked everyone to buy copies for themselves and their friends. I even cheekily suggested that if you were the boss of a business, just imagine what might be possible if your whole workforce read, *How to Be Brilliant*? Then we served more drinks and invited everyone to converse and network.

The first person in the queue bought 200 copies!

The next 10, then 20. The next person bought just one - the cheapskate! (joking), then three and then 60! And so it went on. We sold a couple of thousand copies at the launch. The problem was we'd only ordered 1,000 books. A rush order was placed and the additional copies were signed and sent on as soon as possible. For a new author, this is what's known as a quality problem and a brilliant launch.

Quite different from six friends chatting on Zoom.

You might be thinking, but that's easy when you're selling a non-fiction book; mine is a romantic romp set in the 1600's. Who would want to come to my launch? Simple, invite your Tribe. See Chapter 10.

When you've built a Tribe of people who know, like and trust you and you invite them to your book launch in person or online, they will be thrilled to receive that invitation.

Make them feel special and give them the features, advantages and benefits of your book and why they should also gift it to friends. If it's an online event, make it clear exactly how to order and don't wait until the end to share the link. Then as the orders start to come in, you can check your inbox and thank people by name.

Lots of information there, so let's go through step-by-step how to organise these two different types of book launch.

Don't worry, I haven't forgotten hijack launches.

Physical Book Launch

Find a venue that fits with you and your book. In most cases, a hotel will be too expensive. And, to be honest, they can be quite a sterile environment. Is there somewhere that fits with the personality of your book? How about a small community theatre? Many larger venues have smaller rooms which are perfect for your launch performance.

Or do you have a local library? Libraries are great for book launches. Maybe an independent bookshop? Provided you're happy to give them a decent amount of the profit for hosting, you will often find local bookshops will not only happily oblige, but they will also put your book in a prominent place leading up to and after the event.

Is there somewhere quirky? An old castle? The back room of your local? A little-known cultural hub?

If you have somewhere in mind, I would suggest building a relationship with the owner/decision-maker now, before you're ready to publish your book. Then when you do ask if you can use their venue, not only should you get 'mates rates' (free is always good), but if you've built a relationship, they will be looking after a friend too.

The invitation list should be, in one word, massive. For physical events, even if you've spent some time building your Tribe, assume you will get a one-in-five acceptance and show-up rate. This may seem low, but people are busy and many may not be interested in a launch. Let's break it down. Start with a list of 500 people who you either know or know of and who you would like to invite to your launch. That's a big spreadsheet but it's worth it.

You're going to get a higher hit rate with friends and family, but you also need to think about your wider Tribe and the influencers in your area who you want to invite.

When you invite them, make sure that you give an RSVP. Assume that 20% of those people who RSVP'd 'yes' still won't show up. I know, but that's people.

That's the hardest part done. You now plan to have 80 people coming to your book launch in the back room of the Bear and Treacle pub and it's taking place at 7pm on Thursday.

On the day...

You need to have everything set up and ready by 6pm - at the absolute latest! Having spent many years organising large and small events, I can confidently share with you that there is no better feeling than everything being ready and in place one hour before you're due to start.

Compare it with this. It's your big night and you're frantically trying to make the projector work, organising where people are going to sit, setting up chairs and clearing down tables at 6.55pm. I'm sure you agree that the idea of being set up and relaxed by 6.00pm is glorious.

Next, if you think you have 80 guests attending, put out 70 chairs and have 10 readily available at the back of the room. I learned this routine from attending network marketing meetings in the early 2000's. The hosts who ran these meetings were always good at creating a bit of hype and excitement. The idea of having 'less chairs than audience' means that when the room starts to fill, some people won't have a chair and you (or one of your helpers) will have to grab one from the side of the room or wherever they have been stashed. This translates as 'more people have turned up than were expected'. It works with any number. If you're expecting 20 guests, put out 15 chairs. If you're expecting 200 put out 170. It also means that you don't end up with that embarrassing situation of an empty front row!

Have a host, so you don't need to introduce yourself. Your host should be somebody who will work with you, present you to the audience and say lots of lovely things about you; things that you will have written for them to say.

After you've been introduced, please don't start by apologising. This is a classic mistake where speakers start by saying they're sorry for something: 'It's unfortunate that we are unable to x or y'. I'm not sure of the reason, but authors in particular feel the need to be unnecessarily self-deprecating at this point. Might be a British thing, but it does make your audience think twice about why they're there.

Have your opening statement ready and practice so you can say it without thinking about it. I've found that once you get over those first couple of lines, the rest is much easier. Thank people for coming, but then get straight to the point, your book. Share what it's about and why you've invited the audience. Part of that invitation needs to be why you want them to buy copies and then offer to sign them. Maybe say it's the ideal Christmas, Easter, summer, thanksgiving, any occasion gift, etc but don't shy away from selling.

Remember, if it's a non-fiction book, you can go bigger by asking guests to buy them for their colleagues and staff too.

Sometimes authors have a question-and-answer session. I find that this works best when you have someone to ask you the questions. Effectively you're being interviewed on stage. The interviewer can then open up to questions from the audience. Again, it's one of those occasions that needs some planning. If you suddenly say, does anybody have any questions, and nobody raises their hands, you'll want the ground to swallow you up.

It's not that they don't have any questions. It's that they don't want to ask the first question.

If Richard Branson announces that he's doing an event, and they have a Q&A session, he says, 'I know that nobody wants to ask the first question. So, I'm going to give first-class flights to anywhere in the world that Virgin flies to whoever asks the first question. So, who's got a question?' 95% of the hands shoot up.

I often share that story before a Q&A and add, 'But I'm not Richard Branson. So, what I'm going to do is give a copy of my book to the person who asks the best question'.

It usually gets a laugh and it removes the pressure of the first question.

Be careful not to talk for too long. Remember, you want people to hang around after the event to buy books. If somebody thinks your event lasts from 7.00pm until 8.00pm, and they need to be home by 8.30pm, but you're still rabbiting on at 7.55pm, they'll be counting the seconds until they can get out of there. If your event is due to finish at 8.00pm, make sure your live element finishes at 7.30pm. You should then schedule time to sign copies, talk to guests and ensure everyone has a fun evening. Do that and your guests will stay.

Selling Books at The Event

Make sure it's clear where guests can buy their books and have a separate signing station.

This needs to be done methodically. A pile of books and a friend to take payments. A space where you can sign books. Don't try to be the same person who takes payment and signs books. It slows you down and patience runs out. People will queue longer for a signature than a sale. Always sell first.

Book Bit

Do not use a black ballpoint pen. Don't use a black pen of any description. Black looks like your signature could have been printed inside the book. Whereas a nice fast-flowing blue/green/purple pen looks great when you sign.

If you're unsure about spellings, make sure you have somewhere that buyers can write their name for you to copy. This has happened to me many times before with unusual spellings. 'No, it's not that way, it's Maria spelt with a G!'.

I'll often ask how you spell a name when personalising books, even for some of the obvious ones. For example, 'Jackie', which it would appear, can be spelt in 136 different ways.

Keeping The Flow

You will always get some people who want to have a chat with you while signing. The problem with this is that if you're hosting a reasonably sized book launch, it slows up the queue. So, you need to have a method for moving people on. This isn't being rude; your objective is to meet as many people as possible during your launch.

If anybody buys multiple copies, then make a big fuss of that person. 'Wow, you've bought five, that's incredible, thank you. Would you like me to sign them to individuals, or just sign my name?'

If they have names for individuals, they'll start saying those names. This is good, as other people in the queue start to think about who they might want books signed to. You'd be surprised at how many guests, who originally wanted one book, suddenly switch to three because they think it might be a nice gift for their Auntie Lucy or Cousin Tom.

Online Launch

When you launch a book online, most of the general principles from the physical format remain the same (you don't need to stash chairs though).

If you'd asked me a few years ago about online book launches, I would have been dubious. But since the huge growth of people using programmes such as Zoom, it's now quite common to have meetings featuring people from multiple countries, all in front of their various devices participating in an online event.

You should still have a host who introduces you and you can use the same techniques for generating audience questions. Plus, online guests can ask questions via the 'chat facility', which is more comfortable for introverts.

Other things to consider with online launches are:

Timings

Keep it tight. There's less room for fluff online.

It's YOUR Launch

Remember, this is **your** book launch - YOU need to control it. In the past, I've had members of Write That Book who have left their launch to other members who they met during the programme. On a couple of those occasions, the author didn't know what was happening as the organisers wanted to create 'surprises'. As much as it might have been fun, it meant that the author didn't know the running order, who was saying what and when, plus (and most importantly), there wasn't a natural opportunity for them to sell copies of their book.

Replays

Online events offer the added bonus of a recording. So you can offer a 'watch again' facility.

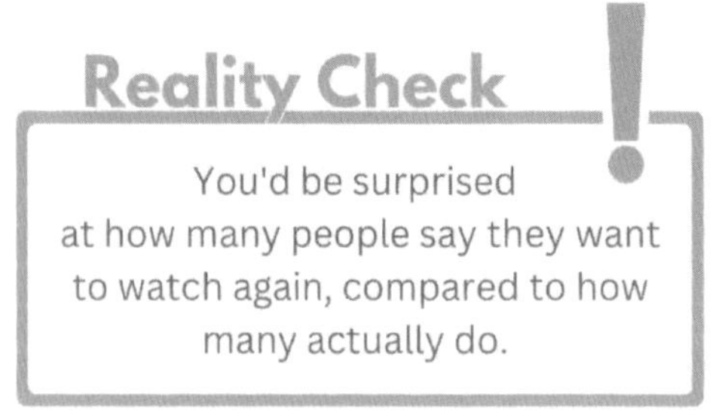

Keep it Simple

Don't spend a huge amount of time on gimmicks, such as music or branded backgrounds. If you're hosting an online launch, you will quickly find this is just something else to think/worry about.

Clarity

When it comes to online events, people like to have very clear instructions. Log on here... This is the password.... It starts at 7.00pm (UK) but you can log on from 6.50pm. We will be finished at X, etc. No matter how good your event may be, people want to know what time it will end.

Make it clear exactly how to order your book.

How to Order

Don't wait until the end before you let guests know how to order. Ask them to order halfway in. This is great when order confirmation emails appear and you can say, 'Oh wow, there's another order just in from Vicky. Thank you'.

Grab a Screenshot

Perfect for your social media accounts. Especially if you have pre-sent books before the launch. Ask everyone to hold up their book and show their copy.

Hijacking Launch

A brilliant way to have a book launch is to hijack somebody else's event. When I say hijack think - be a 'special guest' at their event of course I mean hijack.

If there is something already happening where you know there'll be lots of attendees - and especially if those people are your avatars - then organising a book launch at that event does two things. It enhances what they are doing at their event and it helps to promote what you do. It should be a win-win.

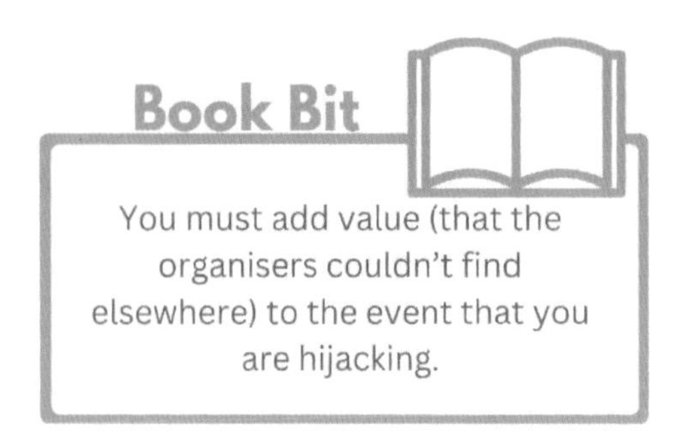

For example, if you've written a book about training dogs, a perfect place to launch this would be at your local Dog Show.

If you've written a book about 50 ways to make your business more efficient, then maybe there's a local Business Club that would love to have you as a speaker. The speaker, who just happens to be launching their book at the same time.

Be a Speaker

There's a brilliant hack, which can help you to sell lots of books, but it may take a little time. It's getting on to the speaker circuit. Yes, if you can get onto a big stage, that's great. Be aware, it's very competitive, so don't worry about moving down a division. There are lots of groups, clubs and organisations who love to have guest speakers. And they're local.

A local author is a brilliant guest speaker and the competition bar is low. The majority of people who speak at these events are usually pretty dull. You won't be. You will create a 20-minute presentation, full of signature stories and offer excellent value for your audience. Your fab presentation will be followed by a 10-minute Q&A and an opportunity for your audience to buy signed copies of your book. You'll leave them wanting more.

The first couple you do will be terrifying, but I promise you will start to enjoy giving talks. And the more you speak, the better you will become and the referrals will follow.

Everything in these recent chapters has been focused on building a Tribe and selling your book. It's tough but worth it. When you start to sell your book to strangers, receive reviews and even make a little profit, it's the best feeling. But you need a product that you're proud of, so now it's time to...

Publish That Book

There is no feeling like it. The joy of seeing your name on the front of a book. It is the most brilliant sensation. You'll always remember the first time you hold your printed book. I have two children and I have to say, seeing my book for the first time is right up there with becoming a parent. It's also amazing how often authors smell their book when it's published. There's something about a new book smell.

With so many routes to market it's worth knowing...

16

Your Publishing Options

What are your options for publishing your book?

I've now written and published nine books. Six, with mainstream publishers (Pearson and Hodder) two of those via an agent and four where I represented myself. I've self-published three; you're holding the third now and I've produced about a dozen audiobooks. I'm not a publisher, so I have no horse in this race or dog in this fight (pick your idiom).

In the past, there were a few simple options. Go with a mainstream publisher, sign with an agent or self-publish. Now, there are multiple routes. I'm going to cover a few and share some pros and cons.

Mainstream (Large) Publishers

Mainstream publishers are the holy grail for authors. However, they are also risk averse and getting past the iron wall is a challenge. But let's be positive.

The Upsides

Size. You'll have a big name behind you, Pearson, Penguin Random House, HarperCollins, etc.

If you're lucky, you will be given an advance. That means you'll have some income while you're writing your book. If you're a superstar, this advance could be millions of pounds. But for new authors, it's usually measured in hundreds. Sorry to burst your bubble. And remember, this is an advance. You'll receive royalties on every copy of your book that's sold, so for the initial sales, all you're doing is paying off the advance.

A mainstream publisher can help with publicity, interviews, etc.

Reach. A huge upside of working with a major publisher is distribution. If you want your book in the famed WH Smith Travel Shops chart, a major publisher is best placed to do that.

International Rights

I've done well with international rights; my books are published in 29 different languages. The idea of negotiating separate contracts for every country where books are published would be impossible for the average author.

Editing Team

This is one of the VERY best things about being with a great publisher; a team (yes team) of people who want your book to be brilliant. From creative developmental editors to fastidious proof-readers, big publishers have amazing talent at their disposal and they are all on your side.

Ego

I've done it. 'Yes, I'm published by Pearson,' I've said. Then unnecessarily adding, 'They're the biggest publishers in the world'. Shoot me now! All ego. But there is something wonderful about having a major publisher believing in you and your book. See Chapter 15 on book launches for more on how you can use this.

The Downsides

Reality Check!

You probably won't get a book deal with a major publisher unless you are already slightly or very famous.

Grrr, I hated writing that Reality Check. I do have the 'probably' caveat in there, but the reality is true. However, I'd love for you to prove me wrong.

I wrote a piece on social media a little while ago about self-publishing. And one of the comments said, 'No way am I going to do that. I'm signing with a major publisher so they will do all the work for me. All I want to do is write.'

Time to burst another bubble. If you write a book and you sign with a major publisher, it will be in your contract that you have to promote the book. This isn't anything new. All writers must (and most want to) be involved with the promotion of their books.

It's hard work. I remember spending hours creating short versions of chapters so that the Marketing Department could send out an abridged version of my books to specialist publications. Some were so obscure I'm not sure whether anybody ever read them.

Remember, the Marketing Department of publishers have multiple books that they need to promote. The ones they are going to work on first are those they perceive will give them a return. Or the ones where they've paid the biggest advance. That means they're publicising authors who are already famous first.

The Money

Another downside of working with a major publisher is you don't get very much money per copy sold. If you earn 15% that means you receive just £1.50 for every book sold at £10.

The other £8.50 is split between the publisher and the retailer. Think about this; you've written the book, will be doing most of the marketing and promotion for the book and you make the least from it. In most cases, companies like Amazon are taking a big slice of the cover price. Another rocket Jeff?

You Lose The Rights

As soon as you sign a deal, you are giving the book rights to a third party. This is the same for any size publisher. That's the deal; they would be crazy to sign a deal and leave the rights with you to sell to another publisher. If you're comfortable with that, great. A particular publisher I had changed the title of one of my best-selling books, negotiated terrible audio rights (meaning I couldn't create audios of my most popular work) and changed book covers without any consultation. That's what I signed up to and there was nothing I could do about it.

On-Demand

At the other end of the scale is print-on-demand self-publishing. Usually, this is done through a provider such as Amazon KDP. This means you carry no stock. You can upload your text straight to the Amazon KDP site and your customers will be able to either buy your book via Kindle or Amazon. This means that when a customer orders your book, they will either receive a digital version, or else just one copy is printed and sent out to the buyer.

As always, there are pros and cons to this type of publishing.

The pros include:

No stock!

You'll never risk being left with a box (or garage) full of books you can't sell - as every book is bought, then printed - meaning it's the most low risk way to publish.

You Set The Price

Amazon has set rates for how much they take and you receive the profit. You can change the price too, meaning if you want to do a crazy 48-hour 99p Kindle sale, you can do so with the click of a few buttons.

It costs you almost nothing

The perfect way to publish without advanced costs and they process payments for you too.

The cons include:

Buying Your Own Book Is Often More Expensive

If you want copies of your book to sell at events or give to friends and family etc, you can buy them from Amazon, but this can work out more expensive than if you printed your own.

Quality

You're limited to size and shape and the quality isn't as good as using a recognised book printer.

Hybrid Publishers

There are various fusion options, where you pay a company to take care of all, or part, of the book's production.

The Pros include:

You can save time and effort. These companies offer everything from editing services, printing, PR and Marketing, stock distribution, you name it, you will find someone who can do it.

The Cons include:

These services come at a cost and there are some (let's call them - less reputable) organisations who, given the chance, will charge you a small fortune and leave you with a box of cheap, often badly printed, books.

Working hard writing your brilliant book, building a Tribe and then paying over the odds for a poorly produced product (when the idea should be to make at least a little profit), doesn't fill me with joy.

Sometimes these companies are described as vanity publishers. I think those days have been eclipsed now by the fact that more people are self-publishing than ever. Many authors choose to self-publish as it is a better route to market for them. However, it's important to know what you're signing up for, who will own the rights, how much you're going to pay for copies and exactly what you'll get for your money.

It's worthwhile taking a step back, having a conversation and asking for some references. Talk to other authors who have used the hybrid publisher route before you make your mind up. I only recommend a handful and you can find their details on the WriteThatBook.co.uk website.

Self-Publish

This is where you do most of the work, but you also get most of the money. And with new technology, it's relativity simple. That's 'simple' not 'easy'.

As usual, there are, of course, pros and cons. This time I've mixed them up a little.

Self-publishing gives you **flexibility**; you can start by publishing this way and move to the other routes. For example, if you self-publish your book and it becomes a hit, you can take it to a major publisher later. You can't do that the other way around.

If you start by publishing your book and print 500 copies, then later want to move to 'print on demand', it's easy to do that. It's more difficult to do in reverse.

You'll most likely want to have your own ISBN number(s). This is a unique book identifier that can be easily turned into a bar code for the back of your book.

With this model you can also print hardbacks, paperbacks and create audio programmes, plus - and here's the exciting part - you own the rights and you get all the profit!

As you can probably guess, this is my preferred method.

I call this the...

17

The Ultimate Publishing Formula

In 2020, when the world locked down, I decided to write a new book; it was called *17 - the little way to get a lot done,* and I managed to take it from idea to book in just 90 days. During the process, I created what I now refer to as The Ultimate Publishing Formula.

You don't need to follow it exactly, just choose the bits you like. Take a little longer than 90 days, but don't deviate too much - this formula is a winner. Many new authors have used it, from memoirs to business books and have enjoyed amazing results.

Here are the major stepping stones (in no particular order):

Set a Publication Date

One that you're sure you'll hit. Authors tend to overestimate what they can do in the short term and underestimate what they can achieve in the longer term. It's important that you're realistic with what you can achieve.

Don't Tell Anyone The Date... Yet

You will want to - but don't. It's important that you make sure your announcement is coordinated. If the news leaks out and your Tribe learns earlier than intended that you are publishing a book on a certain date, and then a couple of weeks later you announce that date, it immediately loses its impact.

Create a 90 Day Plan

Work backwards from when you want to have your book printed and delivered. It doesn't have to be 90 days - that's just the time frame that I used - but it is worth finding out exactly how long each part of the process is going to take and then creating a plan.

Delivery Date

Part of this plan should include your book delivery date. That's delivered. This should be a minimum of two weeks before your publication date. In other words, you should have your books physically in hand, ready to go into envelopes, 14 days before your publication date.

Your Printer

Source a book printer and know your lead times. Everything takes longer than you think.

There are specialist companies who can help you with this. I list some on www.WriteThatBook.co.uk

I would advise that you go with a specialist book printer.

Your mate's cousin who owns the printers on the local industrial estate will claim they can print it, as it's 'just printing and binding' - how hard can it be? However, unless they are printing books regularly, I promise you the quality won't be as good as you wished for.

You want somebody who's going to allow you to upload your copy online, edit it, change sizes, paper types, send out proof copies and give an accurate price. This all needs to be set up.

Know How to Typeset or Engage a Typesetter/Book Designer

I recommend several on my preferred suppliers list at www.WriteThatBook.co.uk

If you like this book, then connect with Matt Bird. He has become my go-to guy for taking words and typesetting them beautifully and publish ready. Let him know you found him via Write That Book for special VIP treatment.

Decide on your Brand and Your Book Cover

I know that you may want to write your book first. But if you're using this formula, it's going to be important that you have your branding ready, so you can build your Tribe and engage your audience in advance of the publication.

The Edit

Make sure you've built in editing time. It's vital, and it always takes longer than you think.

See Chapter 8 on editing for how to turn this chore into a joy.

Now Write That Book

Yes, you have to write it too.

That's the outline of your publishing plan ready, now let's make some money and add...

18

The Ultimate Sales Formula

Selling your book means new readers will give you money in exchange for all your hard work. As you will have worked very hard, doesn't it make sense to sell as many copies as possible?

I think so. The next few pages contain, what I believe, is the ultimate sales formula. I looked at why some authors sold more copies than others and I discovered there were a few golden rules that, when followed, massively increase your chances of selling lots of lovely books.

Build Your Tribe Through Email

The most important part of the sales jigsaw is to have built your Tribe in advance of publication and make members feel part of your community. And you can't rely on social media to do this. That's why I feel it's important to build an email mailing list. Here's how...

Sign up for a free email list platform. I give links to several on www.WriteThatBook.co.uk These are just simple online databases where you can safely store names and e-mail addresses of people who are interested in you and your work. Please make sure that whatever system you use is compliant with the country you live in.

To build your list, I would suggest you offer something in return so that your Tribe members are willing to share their e-mail addresses with you. This must be good value and delight your Tribe member. Delighted means they say with you. Disappointed means they'll click the unsubscribe button.

For *How to Be Brilliant*, I offer new subscribers a free 90-day personal development programme called *90 Days of Brilliance,* which includes videos, audios and regular motivational material. For Write That Book, I offer a fun quiz which identifies the areas an author needs to work on and then follow up with great content and advice. You can review and join both of these groups at www.WriteThatBook.co.uk

Next, regularly send quality content to your list. Remember, don't try to sell anything until you've put deposits into the emotional bank accounts of your Tribe members. That means sending several wonderful emails to your members first. Let them grow to love you!

Pre-Sale

This is where you announce your book is going to be available on a certain date. Because you have taken the time to promote your ideas to your Tribe and you've put lots of deposits in their emotional bank accounts, you've earned the opportunity to ask them to pre-order your book.

This can be done anytime from up to three months beforehand, but most new authors feel comfortable around two months prior.

Ahead of that promotion period, you must ensure that you're going to hit your publication target. That's why you will have created buffers (up to a couple of weeks) here and there to make sure that you are going to deliver on time.

Remember, once you've taken money from somebody (made a sale), you are in a contract with them and you must provide them with a quality product.

Announcements

Announce that there's going to be an announcement. This excites your Tribe about what's to come. They know it's going to be your book, but that's ok.

A week later, make the main announcement. This is where you share that your book is going to be available on X date. And here's the exciting part - you can order it now.

Pre-Order

Give a reason to pre-order. This can be a special offer, a limited run, or maybe something from you as the author. I promoted this book with a hardback copy for the price of a paperback.

Deadline

Set a deadline for pre-orders. You need to know your numbers.

How many books should you print?

When you confirm your book order to your printer, I'd add around 50% to your pre-order number. If you have presold 72 copies, then order 110, if you've presold 400, order 600 etc.

Get Ready To Post

Nothing will prepare you for the potential overwhelm of having to send out piles of books. Set up a system; I use Royal Mail Click & Drop. You can upload all of your orders using a spreadsheet. Then print 'post paid' stickers with all the necessary details and you can even arrange for the postie to pick up your packages which saves you taking them to a Post Office.

When you post your books, send them in good time. A book arriving a little early is better than one a little late.

Reality Check !

Don't set out to make money on postage. Postage and packing should cover the cost of your package and the postage only.

Ask Your Tribe to Publicise

When you send out your books, ask your Tribe to announce that they have received their copies. You can even ask them to publicise if they've pre-ordered it. There's nothing quite like seeing your book in a customer's hand and for them to post a photograph of it.

Make it easy for your Tribe to promote your book; give them the copy (publicity wording), photographs and tell them exactly what you want them to do and when to do it.

Reviews

Seven days after your book has been received, ask your readers for reviews.

There are lots of places to post reviews. If your book is on Amazon, then it's worthwhile asking people to review there, but there are many other book review sites too. Send readers direct links so they don't even need to look anything up.

Have a Launch Event

There's a whole chapter on book launches. You only have one occasion to launch your book, so go for it. Make it brilliant. See Chapter 15.

Sell Through

This means you keep on selling after your initial launch. A good book is timeless. You should be able to continue to sell your book long after it's been written.

You'll see a resurgence in sales of your first book when you publish your second one. New people will enter your world and join your Tribe. Set a target of how many books you would like to sell each year, divide by 10 (yes 10) and set that as your monthly target.

To sell your book, you need it to be catchy, intriguing and simple. That's why it's worth spending some time learning how to...

19

Title That Book

Books need titles. The better the title, the more it attracts your potential reader, cuts through the noise and jumps off the shelves.

This is your book and you can call it whatever you wish. However, you and I know some titles stand out more - and sell better - than others. Your book's title is a huge part of the sales process so it's worth spending some time on it.

Finding a great title can come in a flash of inspiration, or you may have to grind it out. To help you, whether you're flashing or grinding, here's a list of 7 things to consider when choosing your book's title.

1 Is it easy to search?

It's more important than ever that your title is easy to search. Having a title that contains difficult to spell names (or words) instantly reduces the number of people who can find your book.

2 Has somebody already written this book?

There's no copyright on book titles. With a quick search, you'll see if somebody else has already used your title. If they have, it's not the end of the world. If it's already a hit, then leave it. You wouldn't want to publish another Thursday Murder Club. Actually, you'll find that Thursday Murder Club is copyrighted as an entity along with 1,000's of other 'brand' titles. Avoid these at all costs.

However, if another book has the same title, but you're not 'passing off' (as in you're not using the same content), because yours is different and their book isn't a big seller, then you can use the same title.

3 Should it have a subtitle?

Subtitles are often used with business, personal development and other non-fiction books. It helps the reader to understand a little more about your book. A bad title cannot be saved by a good subtitle, but a good title can be enhanced by a great subtitle.

When I wrote *How to Be Brilliant* my editor came up with the subtitle, *Change your ways in 90 days.* I remember reading it and getting the tingles. Since then, I've always looked for a powerful subtitle.

4 Does it need all the words?

Editing your title is as important as editing your book. There's often a load of unnecessary text that can sneak into titles; especially words such as, 'the'. Remove 'the' and see how your book title sounds. Better?

5 Can the title be read on the spine?

Most books are going to be viewed on bookshelves - spine facing. A long, complex title that can't be read is pointless.

6 What's the promise?

In other words, what will your book give the reader? And does your title fulfil the brief?

7 Are you trying to be too clever?

Readers love simplicity. A play on words needs to delight every time the reader picks it up, rather than it becomes a tired pun.

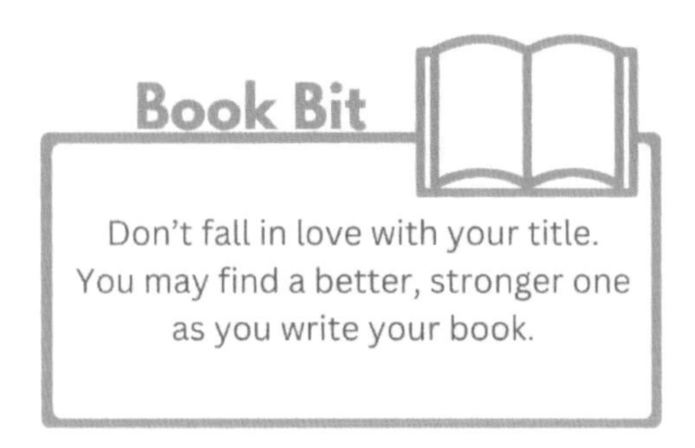

Here are some examples of titles from Write That Book members and authors I've coached, that give the essence of the book in seconds: ***Five Days in Istanbul*** Maisie Sullivan, ***Scared to be me*** Beth Paris, ***Are we there yet?*** Ian Pilbeam and one of my absolute favourites, ***Unsexy Business*** Jamie Waller.

20

How To Pitch a Publisher (or Agent)

Pitching publishers and agents could be a whole book in itself. In fact, my first publisher, Rachael Stock, wrote a very informative book called, *The Insider's Guide to Getting Your Book Published*. Classic gamekeeper turned poacher stuff. It contains every detail you need to know about getting a publishing deal, from the publisher's point of view. But that book was published in 2005 and there have been a few changes since then.

Here's my 'how to'

The big question. Do you really want/need a publisher? If you do want to go down this route, there's a lot of work ahead. Are you up for it? If yes, read on.

Before you waste any time pitching, you must work out who is going to be the best fit for you and your work. Don't be needy, create a mindset of who *you* would like as *your* publisher.

Publishers

You don't need an agent to pitch a publisher, especially in the world of non-fiction. A no-agent (direct) deal is more common in non-fiction than fiction.

Any publisher is going to want to know a lot about you and your idea before they consider looking at a manuscript. This difference is magnified between fiction and non-fiction.

Fiction publishers want to know about you, that you can write and that you've already written the book (or a big chunk of it). With non-fiction, they still want to know a lot about you, but non-fiction publishers would rather you hadn't written your book – just yet. This is so they can work with you on the development side of it.

Let's start with non-fiction publishers.

If I was writing my first personal development book and looking for a mainstream publisher, this is what I would do.

Look at the books you love and check who publishes them.

Narrow this down to a list of half a dozen publishers who you would like to work with.

Google them and find their 'Submission Guides'. No two publishers are the same and neither are their submission guides.

Most non-fiction publishers are going to need this information.

Your Name

Book Title

Subtitle (or options)

Short Pitch (around 20 words)

Long Pitch

Who is it for?

Why will it sell? What problem is it solving? Give a few examples of content.

Metadata (which category or categories would it sit in)

Competitors

Author Biography

How you can help it to sell

Include your number of followers on Social Media – Use your Tribe!

Contact Details

Outline Contents

In the old days, you could print your pitch on fancy paper, send it in the post and hope your 120gsm cream embossed paper stood out. These days, most publishers have an electronic submission form and they insist you use this to send your proposal. Once it arrives, it will probably go to a Junior Editor who has the task (and it is a task) of wading through the 'slush pile'.

Book Bit

As most writers submit their book proposals on a weekend, it means the 'slush pile' is highest on a Monday. If you submit your proposal midweek, it may just land higher up the pile.

All publishers are looking for much more than a good idea. Never forget that publishers are running a business, which means they want to know how you will be part of their success and help them make a profit. That's why they want to know how many followers (easy sales) you have on social media, the number of people on your database etc and what you can do to help sell your book.

Basically, what they're saying is, how can you help us to make lots of money from your book? And that's fine. At the end of the day, the primary purpose of a publisher is to make money and if they make money, you make money. Win/Win

If you have a contact at a publisher, lucky you - don't blow it. It's worthwhile letting them know that you are writing a book. Perhaps ask them for some advice, ask if you can send them your pitch document etc. Give them a heads up, but don't expect any favours.

Fiction and Children's Books

If you're aiming to successfully pitch your fiction idea or children's book, in most cases you're going to need an agent. Don't shout at me - I know I've just said you don't need an agent - but now we're in the wonderful world of fiction and the rules have changed. You'll increase your chances of success if you have an agent. Not 100% of the time, just most of the time.

Agents

Let's look at how you pitch an agent, an agent who will be thrilled to represent you. Literary agents are inundated with new authors. New authors who all think their idea is brilliant. Good agents can sniff out the good ideas from the bad ones in minutes.

Just as you would do with a publisher, you have to make sure your submission to an agent is outstandingly brilliant. Here are some of the key things they are looking for... and some of the disasters you should avoid.

Consider an agent/author relationship as a partnership. You only get out what you put in.

Agents can open bigger gates. If you get over the first hurdle and have a meeting, there's nothing wrong with asking an agent how they would plan to take your book to market.

Agents are looking for long term relationships. What will your next book and the following one be?

Be an expert. Agents want to know that you know your stuff. You cannot do too much research on your subject or be over-confident about it.

Commission

If you're lucky enough to sign with an agent, you must remember that they are going to take a percentage from your percentage of the book sales. Depending on the agent and the amount of work they will be doing for you, this can be between 15% and 20% and they'll receive this in perpetuity.

I've used an agent for a couple of my books; I earn royalties - they earn a commission. Would I use an agent again? Maybe, but only if it was for negotiating high fees between two publishers who both wanted my work.

Good agents are worth their weight as they open doors that you didn't know were there. They can do deals that you could only have dreamt of and will keep you safe in the crazy world of publishing.

A poor agent will do a bad deal, take their fee and do little else. As with anything in publishing and business, be careful. If it doesn't feel right, walk away.

Charlotte Grand is the author of *The Fertility Kitchen*, here's what she did after completing my Write That Book Masterclass. She took her huge collection of cookery books and made a pile of the ones she loved. She turned to the acknowledgements and captured the names of all the agents who were thanked. She then created a master spreadsheet.

She looked at which agents came up most often. Once she'd done this, she updated her spreadsheet and ranked which ones would be her first choice for representation.

She then individually researched each agent and found out what they were looking for and created strong reasons why they would be interested in representing her.

Next, she created a fantastic pitch document for each agent and approached them in turn.

Hard work! Yes, but...

She received an offer from one of the first agents she approached and signed a representation deal. Her new agent took her book to several publishers and she ended up in an enviable position where more than one publisher wanted her book. Her agent was upgraded from 'looking for a deal' to 'negotiating the best deal'.

This is the perfect way to approach an agent and get a book deal. Plus, because Charlotte's book is in full colour as well as a hardcover, it was brilliant to have a publisher behind her who would take care of the expense required to produce a book like this.

Reality Check!

Writing a book doesn't make you an expert. Charlotte had a brilliant idea, is a specialist in her field and had been working on her idea for many years. You need the knowledge before you write a non-fiction book.

There are more publishers than ever and many are wonderful and will help you to take your book to market. But there are some who take advantage of excited new authors, charge a lot of money and provide little more than you could ably do yourself.

Be careful, don't be rushed and remember this is YOUR book. As well as writing and printing your book, why not...

21

Voice That Book

There's no doubt, audio is on the up. Everyone in the book world is talking about audio and with new (free) technology, almost everybody can record good-quality audio.

I created *Voice That Book*, a detailed online 'how to' training programme with Alex Robini. Alex is a brilliant professional voice artist and vocal coach who has voiced everything from commercials to cartoons. I asked Alex, 'Why is audio awesome?' and she shared these five reasons.

Accessibility

Dozens of audiobooks and new audio series are released by the hour. Podcasting has gone crazy with 100 podcasts created every minute. These programmes aren't new, but what's changed is their accessibility. It's never been easier to download and stream audio.

And for the creator, accessibility has opened up too. It's amazing how easy it is to set up a home studio and record your audio.

Mobility

Audio can accompany you everywhere. You can listen to an audiobook while walking, cooking, ironing and even swimming! Audio is the medium for the multitasker.

Adaptability

Audio is evolving. Most genres can now be adapted to audio. Of course, you can listen to a novel, but you can also listen to art exhibitions, personal development coaches, interviews, children's books; if you can read it, you can voice it.

It's down to the imagination of the creator. When you're reading this chapter, ask, 'What could I do with voice?'

Proximity

One of audio's superpowers is the proximity it creates. Listening to someone's book is the door into the writer's imagination, especially when you're listening to the author reading their own words. There's magic when you hear the author's voice; their pace, their rhythm, their accent and their belief. When it's done well the magic shines through, giving the book extra oomph. This authenticity creates a feeling that they're close by and reading their book just for you.

Captivity

When listeners start to play your audiobook, you have a captive audience. It's not the same as spending 20 minutes reading social media or watching YouTube videos, where you can hop around. With audio, you have a captive audience. When accessing written words online, readers can kid themselves that they are able to watch two screens at the same time, but you can't listen to two different audio streams. After a few minutes, your brain would pop.

Plus, you're captive when you're *recording* your audiobook. You may think you're focused when you're writing, but the chances are that you can cope with a gentle distraction - the tv in the background, radio or music - but when you're recording, you must have silence. This leads to a new level of focus.

Awesome Audio Facts

The average Audible member purchases 17 audiobooks a year.

48% of regular audio listeners are under 35. This is a huge growth market.

Recording audio is inexpensive. In the past, authors thought it would cost a fortune to create a quality audio programme. That's because it did. Now you can record and produce good quality audio in the comfort of your own home and it shouldn't cost much at all.

10 Tips to help you record great audio

1 Avoid recording straight after a meal or when you're very hungry. An empty(ish) stomach has the advantage of being discreet!

2 Warm up your voice. Do breathing and vocal exercises.

3 Choose an area in your home that's silent. Be aware of background noises: children, dogs barking, birds tweeting, the washing machine...

4 Avoid distractions: switch off your phone and choose the right time of day for you.

5 Wear comfortable and 'silent' clothes... avoid stiff shirts that might make swishing sounds and avoid dangling jewellery, noisy bracelets etc.

6 Use an iPad/tablet/phone for your text rather than noisy paper.

7 Have water ready – but just take sips.

8 Remember to keep your distance from the mic. Measure 20cm - it's approximately the space between the tip of your little finger and thumb when you open them wide.

9 Use headphones. Always listen to your voice using headphones as it isolates the voice.

   Mouth noises, loud breathing and explosive consonants are easier to spot when you're recording using headphones. Also, it sounds more professional and 'sexy', so it helps to boost your confidence.

10 Remember to smile - this should be fun. Enjoy it! Savour the moment. Listeners can hear a smile.

Questions I'm asked about creating an audiobook

Should I use a narrator?

Alex is a professional voice artist; she believes that we all have the ability to voice our own words and that every voice is suitable for voiceover work. You don't need to have a beautiful voice, you just need to know how to use what you have.

If you do decide to use a narrator, it's worth spending some time finding the right fit. There's a huge responsibility. They're going to give your work its audio identity.

Deciding to use a narrator is a big decision, but before you do, I would challenge you to have a go yourself first. I think you'll be surprised at how good you'll be.

If I do want to use a narrator, where do I find voice talent?

Ask The Google! There's no shortage of talent but what's most important is your relationship with them and this starts with your artist brief. When you ask for audition samples, be specific about what you're looking for; age, sex, accent, pace, dramatic style, etc. They can all be filtered.

Once you narrow your samples down to two or three, ask to have a Zoom call with them to see how you get along. Maybe send them a chapter and ask how they would voice a section or a character.

Should I change my text for the audio version?

When you're recording your audio version, there will be some parts, that on reflection, you'll want to edit. There are parts of the text that you will want to change so that they flow nicely when you're recording it, especially if you've inadvertently written a tongue twister.

If you have a mistake in your book and it's gone to print, you can fix it in the audio. I was happy to record the audio of my book ***17*** as there was a silly mistake on the very first page. Only a couple of people spotted it and both were doing the same thing; listening to the audio at the same time as they were reading the book.

When I first started recording audio versions of my books, I was fanatical about making it word for word the same. Now I believe the audio should be a different (enhanced) version for the listener. When I recorded the audiobook for ***17***, I added two hours of extra material that isn't in the book. I've done the same with this book. If you'd like the audio version, you can find how to download it here: www.WriteThatBook.co.uk

What should you enunciate?

Mainly chapters and headings. Listeners like to know where they are.

Who owns the copyright on audio work?

You do! Anything that you produce, you instantly own the copyright. The key is making sure that people know that. Just as a book has a copyright statement at the front, with audio it's usually at the end. In most cases, if you have self-published, you will own Exclusive Rights. If you've signed with a publisher ask them.

For exclusive rights, just say:
Recording copyright [your name, your publishing company - if you've created one -and the year]
Text copyright [Your name and the year]
All rights reserved.
The moral rights of the author have been asserted.

I hate the sound of my voice.

I think you should give yourself a break. Your voice is wonderful and as unique as your fingerprint. You will get used to your voice in time. The more you practice, the more you'll learn to love your voice.

Why doesn't it sound like me?

It does sound like you. You're hearing a version of your voice that has rattled through your skull and infiltrated your inner ear. It took me several years before I accepted my voice.

What bonuses can I add to audio?

Listeners love to have access to extra content, so it's a brilliant idea to add bonuses.

For a non-fiction book, you can add some of the content that you edited out. Or share with the listener some of the deeper thinking behind your ideas. Fiction authors could do a mini-story or give additional profiles of the characters. And all authors could be interviewed for a bonus 'meet the author' chapter.

How long does this take?

It takes the time it takes. Some authors take to audio quickly and create great content, for others it takes a little longer. Even if you're a professional voiceover artist, you're used to recording at a pace and you don't make many mistakes, it's still a long process because a book is rarely going to be just a few pages long. Plus, you'll want to rest your voice. Even the best voices need a break.

I think for every one hour of finished material, it will take four hours of recording and editing. There's setting up, making sure you're physically and mentally ready, recording, re-takes, editing, tidying up, making sure that you've outputted correctly and uploaded the files to be hosted.

If your book is 10 hours long, plan around 40 hours to work on it. But like writing, once it's recorded it's there forever. Do the work once, then sell it over and over again.

Go on... Voice That Book.

22

Your Call to Action

This is it! It's now time to use everything you've learned and to write, publish and sell your book. As a professional speaker, I frequently suggest to an audience that, 'The secret isn't in the knowing, it's in the doing'. That's why I'm challenging you to ***DO*** what you've learned in this book and to take immediate action. Understanding what you've learned at an intellectual level means nothing if you don't apply the knowledge in a practical way.

When Writing That Book, one of the big surprises is the discovery that the more you learn, the more you realise how much there is to learn. This shouldn't stop you from pushing the button and propelling your writing project over the line. There are three truths that all authors must accept:

You will never know enough

Your book will never be perfect

You will never feel ready

Publish anyway. What would you rather be, perfect or done?

I've set a crazy goal and I hope you'll be a part of it. My goal is to help 1,000 people to write and publish 1,000 books. Let me know when you've written your book. I want to buy as many books from as many authors who have used Write That Book as possible.

It's time to get your book over the line.

23

Bonus Essays

The following pages contain 24 short essays. Each one is designed to stimulate your synapses, pose and answer questions and motivate you to take action. You'll spot several of the ideas from the main content of this book. There was a part of me that thought I should merge it all together. However, my beta readers loved these short essays and agreed they should remain exactly as they are.

Some are adapted from my newsletters; you can subscribe here: www.WriteThatBook.co.uk And some have been languishing on my hard drive, waiting for a polish before publication. A few I've written from scratch.

They could all be described as a good 'loo read'. That's one or two articles to interest you when you're in the smallest room. I hope you enjoy reading them as much as I enjoyed writing them.

Dastardly Dialogue

You can do whole courses on it. Employ an editor just to work on it. But what's the point if you continue to make the simplest dialogue mistakes?

You can tell when an author is trying too hard when every piece of conversation contains an adverb alongside the few words that were said.

> 'I can't be bothered,' she exclaimed breathlessly.
>
> 'Will I see you tomorrow?' he muttered with bemused bewilderment.

You know the type of book? Gosh, it makes a hard read. Instead, just do what the pros do.

> 'I can't be bothered,' said Sue.
>
> 'Will I see you tomorrow?' he asked.

Simplicity speeds up the dialogue. And if your writing is as strong as your reader is smart (they're normally smarter than you think), they'll enjoy the pacy interaction, read faster and enjoy your work much more.

Put More in by Taking More Out

Every day you have amazing ideas. You're wired to be creative, survive and thrive. And I believe you must unlock that creativity in your written work. But how?

One of the best ways to do this is to stop trying to put more in and instead take something out.

Often authors try to put too much in. Doing this is like attempting to be heard in a noisy room. The louder people become, the louder people become. It's hard to be creative when your brain is full and you're trying to add even more. By creating space, you allow the flow of new ideas.

Try taking something out. This could be from your writing or your mind. Both will work. Remove the noise. Breathe deeply. Listen to the space.

A super writing tip is to remove the first sentence or paragraph when you do your first edit and see if it improves what you have written. I often do this with my weekly newsletters. I'd estimate that over half read better *without* the first few lines. This could be because I'm just warming up, or maybe it's because I try to put in too much information at the start; information that the reader doesn't need or could receive later.

Finally, you'd be surprised at how much content you can remove during the first edit, whilst still retaining the essence of your book and engaging your reader.

Counting words because you think a book of your type should be x number of words never works. When I wrote *How to Be Brilliant* I had that mindset.

I remember saying to my wife (and co-author) 'I need to pad out Chapter 3, it doesn't seem long enough.' She disagreed and thought it was fine, but I insisted on adding 2,000 extra words. When my editor returned the manuscript with her editor's pen notes, above Chapter 3 she wrote:

> *There's a problem with the beginning and the end of this chapter. They're too far apart. Suggest losing around 2,000 words.*

The Joys of Copyright

When I interviewed a publishing lawyer for Write That Book Masterclass, it was one of the most anticipated discussions. And lots of worried writers wanted to know about copyright - especially what you can and can't use, do and say.

I've been helping people write, publish and sell their books for several years now and I think I've seen it all.

From writers who are terrified to share even the smallest parts of their work for fear someone 'nicks it', to those who'll happily reproduce a whole song's lyrics and feel nothing about 'borrowing images' from the internet to promote their work through social media.

My take on copyright is simple.

If you don't own it, don't pinch it.

Or, take the time and ask permission. Most writers and publishers will give consent to reproduction, in context, if asked.

As I write non-fiction personal development books, much of my work is used by trainers and coaches. There hasn't been a single occasion, when asked, where we haven't given permission for someone to reproduce our ideas.

So long as they credit the source, why wouldn't you want someone to talk positively about your work and benefit from it?

When you write something original, you own it. The copyright is yours and of course, you want to protect it.

Remember, it's the same for the copyright holder. They want to protect their work too. It's called being fair.

Copyright needn't be complicated.

What's Your Brand?

McDonald's golden arches, the bold tangerine of Sainsbury's, the unmistakable font of Coca-Cola - all iconic. But they are only a part of the brand. They may be recognisable and the easiest part of a brand to imitate, but using an apple doesn't make you Apple.

As a new author, do you need to consider your brand? Maybe it's important. Maybe not. There's no doubt that as a writer, it's harder to be heard in our noisy world. One way to cut through the clatter is to build your brand. And it needn't cost a fortune.

There are a few things that you can do right now to build your personal brand.

1) Be crystal clear on what you stand for

Often people mix up a brand with a logo. I started this message by referencing McDonald's iconic 'golden arches'. We recognise them, they have a clear brand promise. It might not be the best quality food; but it is convenient, affordable and fast.

2) Communicate your message

Do this over and over again, but be focused. You only need to talk to your Tribe. Whether this is publishing stories, creating blog posts, tweeting tweets, curating Instagram memes, designing Pinterest boards, whatever; just make sure you do it consistently. If it's in front of your Tribe, relevant and regular, it's building your author brand.

3) Think about your brand aesthetics

Choose a colour (or a couple) that work well for you and make a note of the 'hex colour code'. Do the same with your font and consider the imagery that best represents you. Websites like Canva will help you to do this.

It's a mistake many authors make, to leave the marketing of themselves (and their book) until the last minute. Usually about a week before publication! Only then do they try to build their author brand, while wondering why they're finding it difficult to sell books.

Don't wait a moment longer. Start to build your brand now.

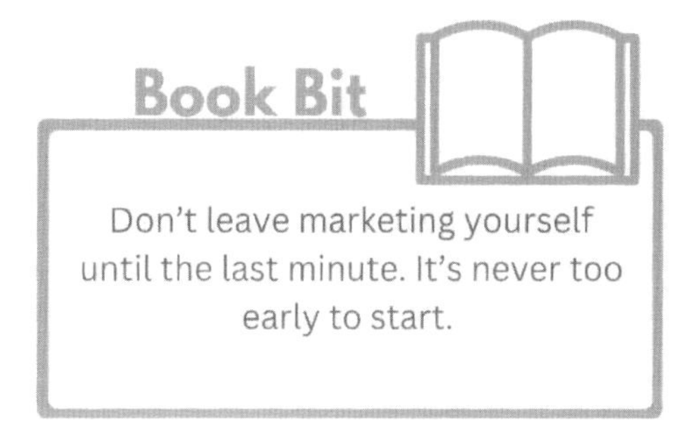

The Top 3 Mistakes Most Authors Make

I wrote this piece several years ago and it has become one of my most-read blogs. I think it's because it's so full of truths.

Mistake 1. They think they're not good enough

There are many stories about authors and rejection. You've heard them and possibly experienced something similar to them. I wonder if that's why so many potentially great authors never write their story.

I'm sure millions of books haven't left the minds of the authors or made their way onto paper for fear of 'not being good enough'. All authors experience this. Whether you're Stephen King, JK Rowling or Agatha Christie, every writer believes, at some point or other, that they're possibly not good enough.

The trick to breaking through these self-doubts is to focus on 'the work'. And the work is writing. One... word... at... a... time. By doing the work, new authors quickly discover that they're much better than they thought. The wedge of doubt diminishes, confidence rises and guess what? You're writing - and writing well.

Here's something you could do right now to overcome the wedge of doubt:

> Write a 500-word essay, paper or short story. As soon as you're done, **leave it** for 24 hours. This 24-hour rest period is essential before you read it back. You'll realise you're better than you thought. Then edit, rewrite and share it with your Tribe. You'll love the feedback.

Mistake 2. They assume you must write the whole manuscript before you sell it or pitch it.

This is a huge and costly mistake; especially if you're writing a non-fiction book. Many publishers would rather you present them with an idea and a sample of your work than with the finished product. They would rather have the opportunity to influence a book than be handed a completed work which needs lots of changes.

Even if you're writing fiction or children's books, there are lots of things you can do to improve your prospect of publication before you've completed your manuscript.

And, if you're self-publishing, you don't need to have finished your work before you tell your story. Start selling yourself and your idea early. If you share from the heart, you'll find your potential buyers (your Tribe) will enjoy accompanying you on the journey.

Mistake 3. They believe the only way to publish is via a mainstream publisher.

This year, 1.6 million books will be published. Only a fraction of those will be via mainstream publishers. Yes, you might land a major book deal. You might get one of those prized cash advances so you can take six months to do nothing else but focus on writing your masterpiece. And then, pigs might fly.

I'm sorry to burst your bubble, but the reality is that most writers are very much part-time, don't have agents or publishers working with them and need to find new and imaginative ways to publish their books.

However...

Hybrid publishing, self-publishing, Amazon KDP, crowdfunding, audio only, POD - Print On Demand and multiple other publishing methods are available to new authors like you.

And once you know how to use these brilliant publication tools, you can produce your work, market it then sell it to your audience.

Would you like one more?

Mistake 3.5 They don't ask for help

It can be a lonely pursuit; writing and publishing your book. So much is trapped in your head. You can't talk to family and friends - they just don't 'get it'. Google searches bring up the titans of publishing but they're out of reach. Don't expect a response from David Walliams if you email him for his take on your children's story. So where to start?

It's important to surround yourself with other people who are also on the journey. New writers, like you, who can share the ups and downs, or the Author-Coaster (see Chapter 4) as I call it. These highs and lows are all part of the thrill ride when you have a group of people who are all on the same journey.

Time to silence Miss Lumsden

When I was 15, my English teacher, let's call her Miss Lumsden, wrote in my final school report... 'Michael will never do anything with the English Language'. That didn't bother me. I was going to be going 'up' in the world! My dad had a roofing business and I was joining it as an apprentice slater and tiler.

Fast forward a few years and I needed to write. I became a youth worker, fundraiser and eventually a professional speaker. All of these required me to produce words. Writing. And yet Miss Lumsden's report kept popping up from goodness knows where. Could I really do this? Am I good enough?

Who's your Miss Lumsden? We all have one. That person who knocked your confidence. That voice deep inside that creates your wedge of doubt. It's time to silence Miss Lumsden!

One day, I realised a simple truth. Miss Lumsden hasn't a clue who I am. What I do. Why I write. I'd bet you fifty quid she has no recollection of writing that school report.

I silenced her there and then.

It's time to silence your Miss Lumsden. You can do this!

The Unexpected Bonuses of Being an Author

When I wrote my first book, I would have been delighted if my Mum and a couple of others, had bought it. All I longed for was my name on the cover of a book.

Just a few weeks after publication, *How to Be Brilliant* entered the top ten best-selling business books and stayed there for two years and four months.

Wow! My life changed.

I wasn't a celebrity author - I didn't want to be, I'm quite a private person, but here are three things that happened because of my first book:

I was able to significantly increase my fees as a speaker and coach.

Celebrities approached me to coach them; Davina McCall, Sara Cox, Patrick Kielty, England footballers and even a supermodel came into my world because of the book.

My confidence in my ability soared! I was no longer just Michael Heppell; I was now Best-Selling Author, Michael Heppell.

Something similar happened to my fellow authors who are fiction writers (upgrades, invites, connections) and it often happens to children's authors too.

I'm not suggesting you need, or want, these things. What I am saying is that writing and publishing your book is an amazing catalyst in helping you to achieve any goals you might have.

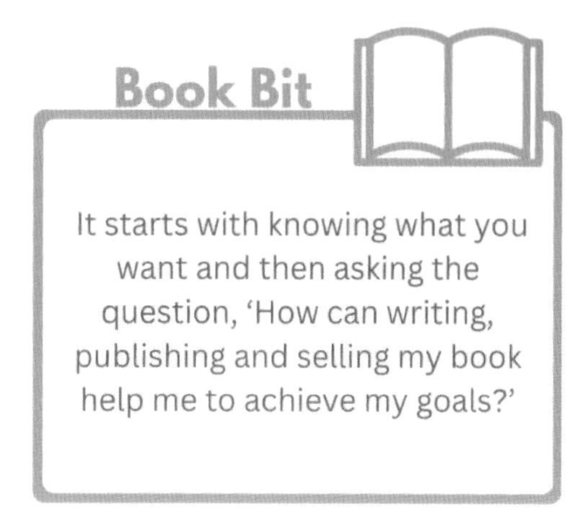

Know Your Niche

In 1848, James W Marshall discovered gold at Sutter's Mill in Coloma, California. Prospectors in their thousands (300,000!) were drawn to the heart of the action. The Gold Rush!

Some panned rivers, others just started digging and a few blew up mountains. And the smart ones invested in working with geologists to discover the most likely place to find a seam. If they were lucky, it meant riches beyond their wildest imaginations.

Very few of the panners, random diggers or blasters did find those riches. There was a much higher reward when working with a geologist. By using specialist knowledge, they were more likely to find a seam of the illusive mellow yellow metal.

Finding your niche is like discovering a seam of gold. A ready-made audience who love what you do and more importantly, want to be part of it. This is truly finding your Tribe.

In my Write That Book Masterclass, I coached Heather Stevens. She's an amazing dog trainer and is now a published author. She wrote a brilliant book called '*Beyond The Breed*'. It's not a book for dog lovers, or even for dog breeders. It's a specialist book for dog trainers.

She was always regarded as an expert. But the moment she published her book she became the authority [Author-ity].

Heather has received speaking invitations, the opportunity to sell books to large groups and is now the go-to person in this niche area.

Book Bit

What's your niche?
You do have one and when you connect your expert knowledge to your specialist audience, you'll have found your seam of gold. All you need do, is mine it.

Spider-Man

Imagine you're interested in comic book superheroes, especially Spider-Man. Your chosen method to connect with other enthusiasts is to wander around Birmingham City Centre, fingers crossed, hoping you will bump into someone willing to trade Spider-Man facts.

It's not looking too promising.

Meanwhile, just down the road, at the NEC (National Exhibition Centre), *Comic-Con* is taking place.

It's packed with thousands of weird and wonderful superhero fans, just like you. Enthusiasts who are happy to talk Spider-Man, Cat Woman and Moon Boy for hours. They love it - costumes and all.

But you still need to reach out.

Just hoping someone might walk up and start that conversation isn't enough, even when you're surrounded by fans and followers. You have to say hello.

Think of it like this:

- Birmingham is the internet
- The NEC is Facebook
- Comic-Con is Facebook Groups
- Engaging in conversation is making a post

There are hundreds of Forums and Groups that specialise in every type of writing, genre and book. Some are better than others. Look local, there may be something just down the road. Ask The Google. You'll find some.

If you're looking for a starter, join my groups. I'm biased, but it is the best and most supportive you'll find by far.

Here's the link: www.WriteThatBook.co.uk

Book Bit

When you join a group, join in. Leave comments, make a post, ask questions, offer support and advice to others and become part of the community. You might even find some Spidey fans.

That Difficult Second Album

You know the band who smashed it with their first album and then found it difficult to do the follow up? Their record company is screaming: do it again, give us more hits!

So why can't they repeat the magic?

Possibly because their first album may only have taken two months to record but... they'd been working on it for the last five years, playing the songs live, night after night. Desperately trying to be noticed. Tweaking their tunes in front of hundreds of critical audiences.

Eventually signing the deal and turning graft into hits. Then they tour the album. Their fame is growing. Those same songs they played to 15 people are now being performed to thousands and their fans are singing back to them. They love it! But the pressure is on. Can they produce something that had previously taken five years and perfect it in five months?

Writers are presented with a similar predicament. Their first book is the one they worked on for years - usually in their heads before eventually committing it to paper. But their best work often comes later.

Ken Follett wrote several books while working as a night security guard, this was long before 'Eye Of The Needle' became a huge success. He explained that he had to write the other books to realise that people don't care about the plot until they care about the characters.

Almost everyone has heard of Dale Carnegie's *How to Win Friends and Influence People*, but how many of his 14 other books can you name?

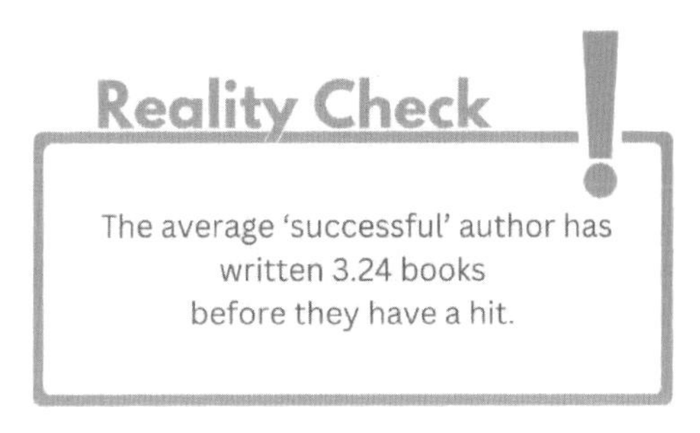

The key? Writers must keep Writing. Testing. Sharing. Learning. And never stop.

There are some exceptions. Emily Brontë only wrote one book, Wuthering Heights.

But did she need another one?

By the way, did you know Emily Brontë self-published that classic?

What's That Smell?

When you open the box and take out the first copy. It's not just the look and the feel of your book that's intoxicating... it's the smell. A box of newly printed books smells amazing. Especially when they're yours.

I know new authors who have kissed their first copy - I did!

But you don't get to smell your book... until you've published a book. And you don't get to publish a book until you've written one. And you don't get to write one unless you find the time.

I'm a big fan of multi-sensory goal-setting. The idea of not just visualising, but hearing, feeling and sensing yourself achieving the goal. And that includes the smell. Mmmmmm.

However, the brutal reality is that thousands of writers won't get their idea from brain to screen, never mind into a printed book. I've two ideas that will help though.

Ask yourself; what is the exact date when your book (or the next one), will be published? The more specific the better. Go for it and schedule the date. Do it now.

Next...

Make yourself accountable. Share with others your book publication date. The moment you post this on your Facebook page, your blog or Instagram feed, you're much more likely to achieve it. I'm passionate about this as a make-it-happen motivator.

Do it and do it now.

This 'deadline' method of goal-setting has worked for thousands of writers, to encourage them to take action. And that's the difference between 'idea' writers and published authors. ACTION.

I love Accelerator Weekends, a time when dozens of writers, just like you, come together and spend two days pushing their projects over the line.

Taking action and being accountable, from finding a publisher to writing 10,000 words, completing the first edit, to setting up a social media campaign.

From finding a publisher to writing 10,000 words, completing their first edit to setting up a social media campaign.

Using Pain as a Motivator

You've just read about setting goals, the incredible emotive smell of your newly printed book and the importance of taking massive action. Now I'd like to introduce you to pain – and especially pain avoidance.

Regret is a horrible word. I don't know about you, but I don't want to leave this world with regrets. Setting the goal is the easy part. Achieving the goal is tough. Those who don't achieve their goals (through quitting) end up with regret.

But have you noticed how they justify this with excuses?
'I was too busy'
'I wanted to make sure my idea was fully formed before I started to write'
'It looks like someone else is writing about...'

This is because, making 'why I didn't' excuses is easier than writing the book.

I believe YOU can achieve most things you put your mind to, especially writing your book.

When I developed my Write That Book Masterclass, one of my favourite interviews was with book marketing expert, Mike Alden. There's a brilliant quote from Mike that sums up the difference between those who 'talk a good game' and those who do something about it. He says more in a motivational 11 seconds about eliminating excuses than I ever could.

'If you did write a book, whether it's self-published or not, congratulations - it's a big deal. Because a lot of people say, 'I have a book in me, I'm going to write a book'. And you can say, 'Well you didn't and I did.'

Compare that with, 'Yep, me too, I'm *going* to write a book'. Fine if you're just starting your journey, but how will you feel if you're still saying that five years from now?

No regrets. Write That Book.

Book Blasts And Asks

You always remember your first Book Blast. The promise is that you will catapult your work to the top of the charts by encouraging everyone to buy your book on the same day, at a specific time.

I've had a couple of successes doing this, but also a couple of catastrophic failures.

One of the flops was when I faithfully promised my publisher that I would sell 5,000 copies in a day and barely managed 500. A plate full of humble pie for me.

However, when a book blast does work, it can help set your work apart from the thousands of other books that were published that day.

Mike Alden (mentioned in the previous pages) is one of the 21 Masters I interviewed for my Write That Book Masterclass. He's brash, straight-talking and certainly lives up to the title of his book, *Ask More Get More*. And he's a Book Blast specialist.

He suggests the top reason most book blasts don't work, is that the author is frightened to ask enough readers to buy their book at the specific time. They're terrified that they may say 'no'. I get that, but if you've worked hard, built a Tribe, given great value and have enough deposits in the emotional bank accounts of your Tribe, there's no reason why you shouldn't ask your followers for a favour on that day.

They might say 'yes'.

When you're publishing your next book, if you want to fire it up the charts with a book blast, start planning now. Make it abundantly clear what you want your Tribe to do and when you want them to do it.

It will normally go something like this - Please buy my book between 6.00pm and 7.00pm on Tuesday 14th. I'm aiming to boost it up the chart and need as many people as possible to buy it then. If you send me your receipt, I'll send you [add something wonderful here that can be delivered electronically] and will be eternally grateful.

Then... ask, ask and ask again.

Reality Check !

Book blasts should only be used for legitimate books and promotions - not for claiming 'best seller' when a book has topped a random chart for an hour.

Why Writers Quit

It was difficult for me to type that headline as I'm known for being a very positive person. You've heard the BS. Usually screamed by larger-than-life motivational speakers, 'Winners never quit and quitters never win'.

Yawn.

That's fine if you're in the middle of a triathlon and quitting would be public, embarrassing and catastrophic.

However, it's not the same for writers. Writers are usually isolated. Working on their words, in a quiet space with little input from others. Quitting is easy for writers. Because nobody knows.

Something that hits home when I talk to new authors, is the number of times I hear words like, 'Always wanted to...', 'I've started so many times', 'I've been writing this book off and on for...'

It's easy to see why writers quit.

What's the secret sauce that stops quitting?

Camaraderie and Accountability.

I bet you'd write your book and hit your target if you had a major book deal, contract and hefty advance. If you miss your deadlines, you let others down and risk being sued. It's quite the motivator. You may have just read something about pain avoidance as a motivator.

That's accountability, which is okay for the short term but in the longer term, you need something a little more positive.

The writing community is one of the most supportive I've known. There's little competition and lots of people who want to help and support you. Those with more experience happily share and those with less experience happily care.

There may be a local writer's group in your town. If not, there are dozens online and there will be a perfect one for you and your genre.

Once you're involved with a supportive network, you will want to get your book over the line and join others doing the same. You'll find it more difficult to quit (although the temptation will still be there), as there's usually someone who will encourage and support you at just the right time.

+Spoiler Alert+

Have you ever read a review and suddenly +SPOILER ALERT+ appeared in the text?

Only for the next few words to read...

He's actually dead.

...and kill the plot.

You have seen Sixth Sense? Whoops.

I have a +SPOILER ALERT+ for you.

If you don't want to know what's about to happen to your book-writing journey, please stop reading this now.

Still here? Good.

You won't write your book.

Ouch.

Or I should say, you won't write your book if you keep on doing what you've always done. Planning, hoping and 'one daying' isn't enough. Time for a plot twist.

This is where the writer pulls it out of the bag, learns the tools, does the work and YES they become a published author and win *The Booker*!

What changed?

All good books need a story arc. And alongside the lows, there should be some epic highs. Where are you on your arc? And what's next?

In most good plots, what is it that changes the tempo?

It's when the hero decides enough is enough. There's a moment when the shift happens.

It's often around the same time as when the shit happens. For an author, it's when their mindset goes from, 'I'm going to write my book' to, 'I am writing, publishing and selling my book!'

That's a plot twist.

What Links Authors, Brushes and Cinnamon?

November 1st is their National Day.

Along with: Vinegar, Deep Fried Clams, Biological Coordinators (?) and 'Cook for your pets'(!) who all celebrate their special day on November 1st.

The history of National Authors' Day

In 1928, Nellie Verne Burt McPherson - what a name - president of the Bement, Illinois Women's Club, had an idea of setting aside a day to celebrate authors.

She was recuperating in hospital and wrote a fan letter to fiction writer, Irving Bacheller. She told him how much she enjoyed reading his story *Eben Holden's Last Day A' Fishin*.

Bacheller sent her an autographed copy of another story and Nellie decided to show her appreciation by submitting the idea for a National Author's Day 'to observe and honour writers'.

Beat that cinnamon, brushes and cooking for pets!

Today, readers are encouraged to reach out to Authors and let them know how much they have enjoyed their work.

And authors melt.

Book Bit

Writing a book is brilliant.
Receiving a review is magical.
A personal message from a reader is the most beautiful thing.
But first, you must write, publish and sell your book.

What's The Point?

Is it worth it? The time, the effort and the energy? Is there a point? You know I'm going to say yes. But why?

I started this book with: 'It's not the book you read that will change your life. It's the book you write.' By now I'm hoping that I've convinced you that you can do it. It's difficult to put into words, the feeling when you hold your newly published book. Your work, with your name printed on the cover. And here's the point.

YOUR BOOK WILL BE HERE FOREVER!

One of the best things about writing, is that once you're finished, your work keeps on giving. Long after you've typed those final words,

The End.

In 2020, when the world first 'locked-down', sales of my book, **Flip It** - *how to get the best out of everything,* soared. It was first published in 2009, yet the promise became more important than ever that year. *Flip It* was there to help and will still be around long after I've gone. Your book will be too.

Another point is that you answered a call to discover more about writing. You're reading this book. You're an author. You must write, publish and sell your book. That's a **must**, not a should. Non-writers don't get it.

And that's the point.

Scrappy, Idea or Starter?

These are all author types.

Scrappy Writers
Idea Junkies
Super Starters

All writers have some good ideas and some bad habits. Some have lots of bad ideas but drive through with good habits. Some manage to keep their bad habits low and their good ideas high. And for many others...

It's their bad habits that are the barriers to them becoming successful writers. They didn't plan to develop bad habits. No one does, it just happens.

Scrappy Writers write a few words here and there... but never write their book.

Idea Junkies seem to have half a dozen 'concepts' on the go... but never write their book.

And Super Starters have first pages aplenty... but never write their book.

To Write That Book you may need to build some new habits. They're all in this book. When you read it again, ask yourself if you know it or do it? Knowing is good, but won't get your book over the line. It's regular action - habit building - that makes the difference.

It's time to Write That Book

There's More to Life Than Amazon

It's the biggest bookshop in the world. Actually, it's the biggest *everything* shop in the world.

There's a strange relationship between authors and Amazon.

Love and hate
Yin and Yang

'Available on Amazon' is part of every consumer's vernacular.

But there's more to life than Amazon.

Independent Bookshops

We all want to support independent bookshops. The best way to encourage your local bookshop to stock your book, is to buy books from your local bookshop. Encourage others to support them and champion their name on your social media. If they agree to stock your work, let friends and followers know that that's the shop where they can buy your book.

Supply Direct

There are loads of ways for you to sell books directly to your readers. It's never been easier to set up a simple website with a sales page. You can even connect it to Royal Mail to print your postage labels and arrange for them to pick up your parcels!

You don't need Amazon to sell your book online.

Sell, sell, sell!

I believe authors need to engage in a little sales hustle.

I don't mean that you need to go all *Wolf of Wall Street*, but having the confidence to set up a simple sales page, support and approach local shops and make your work easily available, must part of every author's journey.

Partnerships

Who do you know that would be a good fit as a partner? Someone or somewhere that would be great to stock your book? If you are going to ask someone to be a partner, go into the relationship with a 'give to get' approach.

That means, you help and support them first. Yes, we're back to putting deposits in the emotional bank account.

Reality Check!

Amazon is brilliant.
Their customer service is excellent.
Their marketing budget is massive.
And their infrastructure is mind-boggling. So yes, use them, but don't rely on them.

Price That Book

Pricing books is a difficult science. You don't want to put potential readers off, but you do want to make a few pounds for your efforts. How do you get it right?

I've observed these three mistakes.

Mistake 1

Most writers under-charge for their books. It's a confidence thing.

Authors who write specific technical books can charge hundreds per copy. They know their worth and that their readers are paying for knowledge, rather than the paper it's printed on.

Something to think about?

Mistake 2

Many writers make the error of thinking their book is for everyone, when it may only be for 1% of the population.

However, that 1% is still 670,000 in the UK alone!

As a first-time author, I'd be happy with just 1% of the 1%. I love these statistics as it shows you can target readers and (here's the best bit) talk to them directly.

Mistake 3

Not building and investing in your audience.

Without deposits in your reader's emotional bank accounts it's difficult for them to part with even a few pounds from their monetary bank account.

When you have members of your Tribe asking when your book will be available, you know there's a ready-made audience itching to buy your book. That gives a wonderful feeling of confidence to a new author.

Reality Check!

You probably won't be selling your book for hundreds of pounds, but I'm sure you can sell it for more than you think.

It's Obvious

There's a book which has sold 18 million copies and is described as 'obvious'.

I bet you've browsed the bookshop shelves and thought, 'Who buys this stuff?' Closely followed by, 'My idea is better than that!' I know I have.

Obvious to you and I may not be obvious to others.

As a writer, it's not your job to create unique. It's your job to write what your readers want to read and will enjoy reading. And I'm not talking about 'selling out' and being the lowest common denominator commercial (as tempting as that may be).

Ken Blanchard and Spencer Johnson wrote the classic, *The One Minute Manager* in 1982. I've read it several times and recommended it to hundreds of people. A couple of years ago I was talking to a business coach who said, 'But it's just common sense. There's nothing special in there.'

Yes, it is common sense, but it's brilliant. They put that common sense into a book. And that's the difference. 18 million copies sold and it continues to sell well.

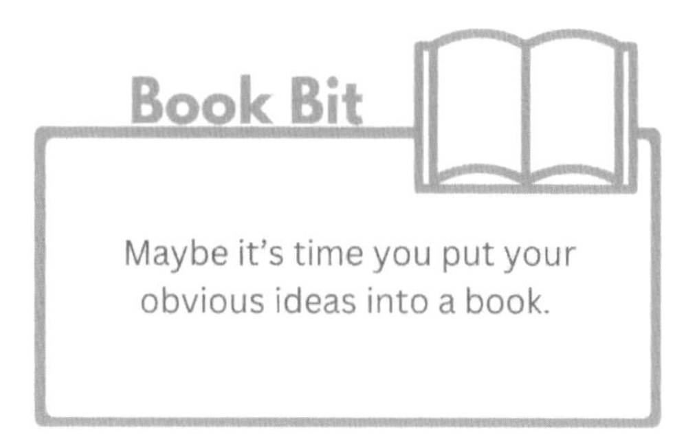

Pushing The Publish Button

Sooner or later your book needs to be published.

Scary! How do you get rid of the fear of publishing your work? The simple answer is you don't.

ALL authors are riddled with fear and self-doubt. Members of my Write That Book community know it's one of the most commonly discussed topics, 'Am I good enough?'

You are, by the way.

I wonder how many books are still hidden on hard drives or trapped in notebooks because the brilliant author didn't dare to publish? I know of several would-be authors who have been writing their books for over 20 years and still they're tweaking; waiting for it to be 'right', while their book remains unwritten.

It's bonkers. But to some degree, we all do it. Whether it's a delay of a day, a week, a month or a year, we're all guilty.

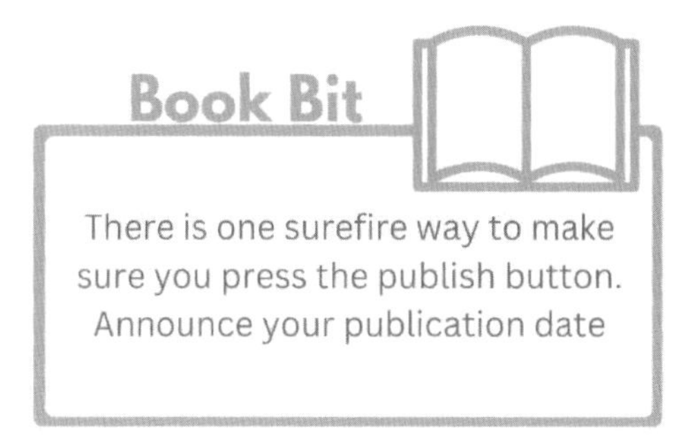

The second you say that your book will be published (on a certain date), you're committed. When that date is out, then it's real. Choose the date, then tell your friends, family and anyone else who will listen.

You'll stay up late and wake up early. You'll turn down invitations for a lazy lunch, choosing instead to edit your work. You'll forget you own a tv! And you'll Write That Book.

What's your publication date? It doesn't matter if it's a month from now or a year - you need one. Otherwise, you'll be reading this book a year from now still looking for the confidence to push the publish button. As soon as you commit, you make it a must.

Publish That Book!

Is My Book Too Long?

I get asked this question often. My simple answer is:

'Never too long, only too boring. Never too short only too sparing.'

I give the same answer for chapters and paragraphs.

If you're writing a novel, you must ensure your reader has invested in your characters. This takes time and a lot of effort. Characters should lead the plot, so don't skimp on them. If I don't care about your characters, I won't want to read about them, no matter how good your plot is.

If you're writing a non-fiction book, then you must create value. I'm amazed (and get p***ed off) at the non-fiction author who decides to leave the best stuff out of their book, hoping that readers will be lured into buying other products 'to find out more'. Your best stuff should be front and centre.

Memoirs can be self-indulgent. What you think is an interesting story, that takes you 3,000 words to tell, could be a page-skipping bore for your reader. As a rule of thumb, 25% of memoir stories should be seriously edited or taken out of the second draft.

Children's books should be easier, but every single syllable needs to earn its place. In the children's market, you have two customers you're writing for, the child and the reader/parent.

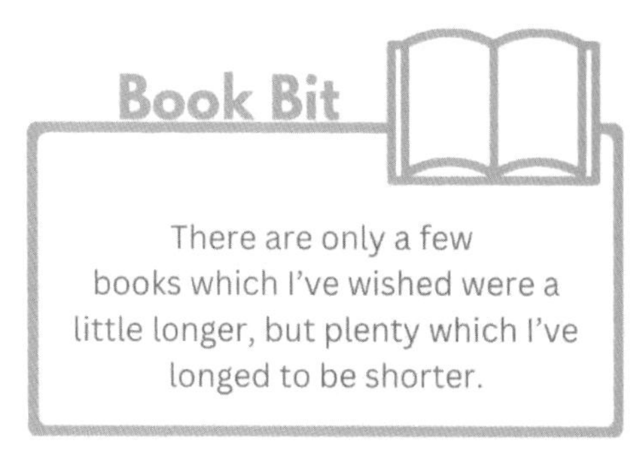

Your Place in The London Marathon

Let's assume (for some bizarre reason) you decide to run the London Marathon. You apply and - shock horror - you win a place. But you don't have a plan. Now all you must do is train for and run a marathon safely. How hard can it be?

Which preparation method do you think would work best for you?

Fall in to a personal 'work it out as I go along' programme, toil on your own and just battle through?

Or...

Join your local, *Get fit for London* running club?

What happens next?

The marathon doesn't take place for six months, so you can put off your training for a little while. Maybe wait until the nights become longer and lighter?

And if you want to miss a few sessions... who cares? Then you skip a couple more as it's a bit cold and wet. You convince yourself that a marathon can't be that hard because you've seen people run it in a chicken costume.

You assure yourself it'll be fine, quit the boring training and decide to just rock up on the day. What's the worst that could happen?

Don't answer that.

Or you join *Get fit for London,* where the promise is; to take you from couch to marathon safely in 5 months'. They do this by using their secret weapon.

It's a club.

This means that on the days when you don't want to train, you will. When you're feeling a little low, a fellow GFFL club member is going to pick you up. And on Marathon day, when you don't think you have anything left, you'll dig deep - because you're running as a team.

The good news is, this is just an analogy. You don't have to run the London Marathon - phew. But you do have to write your book.

I've just described a writer's *Accountability Group*. For many Write That Book members, it made the difference between years of wanting to be a published author and writing, publishing and selling their book.

If you'd like to join an Accountability Group, you can find one here: www.WriteThatBook.co.uk

End This Book - The Final Bit

Writing a book called *Write That Book* should have been easy. It's a subject I've been teaching for years with one-to-one coaching clients, hundreds in masterclasses and pop-up groups with over 1,000 members.

I've written nine books, from a popular Sunday Times Number One Best-seller (*Flip It*) to a book so niche that unless you are a manager in the world of further education you would never have heard of it (*Future Proof Your College*).

My books have been published in 29 languages and are sold across the world. I've given hundreds of interviews about writing and written millions of words. It's a passion.

But writing *Write That Book* wasn't easy. My biggest challenge was what to put in and what to leave out. What's current, but could change between now and going to print and what's timeless, but too obvious?

My mind became obsessed with how much is enough. Could I delve into using artificial intelligence for idea generation? I chose not to. Should I give tips on advertising? Again, I decided no, thinking most authors like free (Tribe building!).

How much space do I give to selling a book vs writing style? Looking at the number of 'How to write' books vs 'How to sell what you've written', I think I've helped to fill a gap.

I've searched for a balance, but I am aware this is far from a complete guide for every author.

As with my courses, I knew some readers would be writing their tenth book and others would only have the seed of an idea. Where to pitch it?

In the end, I took my own advice, looked at my core values and beliefs and wrote from the heart.

I hope you've enjoyed reading it as much as I enjoyed writing it and you're more committed than ever to *Write That Book*!

Michael Heppell
www.WriteThatBook.co.uk

Acknowledgements

There are so many people to thank for helping me to Write That Book.

First and foremost, my amazing wife, editor, co-writer, constant critic and biggest supporter, Christine.

Vanessa Thompson, who has been the third Musketeer and greatest friend. Thank you for taking on the epic task of the first copy edit.

The newest member of the Michael Heppell team, Sarah McGeough who is the epitome of diving in.

Matt Bird, the most patient man on the planet who made this book look fabulous, pointed out some glaring mistakes and suggested some wonderful content.

The amazing **Write That Book Admin Team**, who never tire of supporting members and answering questions; Victoria Wilson-Crane, Ian Pilbeam, Roger Wilson-Crane plus Sarah and Matt again!

Thank you to the incredible members of the Write That Book Masterclasses. By teaching you, you made me better:
Adrienne Green * Alan Rafferty * Alex Robini * Alie Calvert * Alison Donovan * Alison Drasdo * Alison Messom * Alison Timms * Alistair James * Alyson Storr * Amanda Payne * Amanda Phillips * Amar Karim * Amber Horrox * Andrea Ince *

Andree Currie * Andreea Sandu * Andrew Mosley * Andy Gilbert * Andy Kenna * Angela Graham * Angela Morris * Angie Beeston * Ann English * Ann Gash * Ann-Marie Ferguson * Anna Anderson * Anna Bravington * Anna Chapman * AnnA Rushton * Anne Goodridge * Annemarie Munro * Annette Brown * Audrey Macnaughton * Avril Owton * Belinda Bond * Belinda Smith * Beth Jordan * Big-Ian Donaghy * Brenda Hector * Carol Andrews * Carol Ann Robinson * Carol Murray * Carol Pollard * Caroline Owen * Carolyn Parry * Carolyne Collins-Atkins * Catherine Pearce * Catherine C Neary * Ceri Goodrum * Charlie Hastain * Charlotte Erika Walker * Charlotte Ord * Charmaine Host * Chris Nichols * Chris Wardle * Christine Beech * Christine Errico * Claire Cattel * Claire Dalgarno-Todd * Claire Guichard * Claire Randall * C E Bland * Clare Fleerackers * Clare Foreman * Clare Fryer * Clayton Doyle * Daniel Altmire * Dave Barker * Dave Jeal * Dave Young * David Gleghorn * David Rogers * David Viner * Dawn Dobson * Dean Coulson * Debbie Bias * Debbie Buxton * Debbie Johnson * Debbie Mitchell * Deborah Brown * Deborah Rogers * Debra Murphy (aka Mother Murphy) * Dee Holley * Dennis Conlon * Derek Crysell * Desiree De Beer * Diana Muzzall * Diane Wyatt * Diane Hull * Diane Parker * Donna Clark * Donna Joseph * Dr Rhona Morrison * Elaine Allen (aka Catherine Cliffe) * Elaine Good * Elaine Wallace * Eleanor Baggaley * Liz Tomkins * Elly Calaby * Emma Hookey * Emma Carter * Emma Nicholson * Erica Sorrel * Erika Beumer * Fiona Gubbins * Fiona Myles * Fiona Setch * Flo Kingfisher * Fran Kruc * Frances Mackintosh * Fraser Newhouse * Gail Hitchens * Gail Molyneaux * Gary Sargent * Gayle Hubble * Gaynor Cherieann * Gemma Crampton * Gill Heppell * Gillian Neish * Gillian Westlake * Hannah Lloyd * Hannah Powell * Hazel Wheatley * Heather Coppard * Heather Stevens * Helen Askey * Helen Cameron * Helen Johns * Helen McCann * Helen Overton-Smith * Hilra Gondim Vinha * Ildiko SpinFisher * Irena Peel * Ishy Bruce * Jackie Watson * Jackie Winnell * Jacqueline Buckman *

Jaki Lewis-Thompson * James Brindley * James Corrigan * James Palmer * Jan Greetham * Jane Brady * Jane Eckford * Jane Geffin * Jane Parsons * Jane Roskell * Janet Ratcliffe * Jean Fleming * Jeannie Duncanson * Jeff Caplan * Jeff Matthews * Jenni Moses * Jennifer Flint * Jenny Williams * Jess Walker * Jill Morris * Jill Savage * Jilli Moult * Jillian Stout * Jinny Morgan Lewtas * Jo Farragher * Jo Hemming * Jo Laking * Jo Ogden * Joachim Buaro * Joanne Bennett * Joanne Conway * Jodie Fairclough * John Alfred Kingdon * John Acton * John Drysdale * John McHale * John G Needham * Jon Asquith * Julie Betterton * Julie Bryant * Julie Jones * Julie Larkin * Justin Turner * Justina McGillivray * Karen Morley-Chesworth * Karen Balmond * Karen Black * Karen Lucas * Karen Mccann * Karen Wagner * Karen Young * Karina Sexton * Karl Perry * Karrie-Ann Fox * Kate Joels * Kate Rodwell * Kate Welch * Kath Cockshaw * Kath Shadnia * Kathryn Brennan * Katrina Reilly * Kay Dobson-Bennett * Kaye Patten * KC Chamberlain * Kellen Ann * Kerry Crichton * Kevin Harvey * Kevin Walsh * Laura Hastie * Lee Naylor * Len Rayne * Lenise Page * Lesley Graham * Lesley Renault * Liam Kirk * Linda Anne Archer * Linda Nightingale * LBW Dancing * Lis Ainsworth * Lisa Berrett * Lisa Carelse * Lisa Gibson * Lisa Jenner * Lisa Kemp * Lisa Leonard Peel * Liz Hughes * Liz Pert-Davies * Liz Tomkins * Liz Welham-Daly * Liza van Linder-Quintos * Lorna Clark * Lorna Vyse * Lorraine Toner * Louise Rogers * Louise Skinner * Lucas Vigilante * Lynn Morland * Lynn Pearson * Lynne Given * Maggie Hart * Maggie Sullivan * Manj Kalar * Maria McCormack * Maria Rowlandson * Maria White * Marian Hackett * Marie Howarth * Marilyn Payne * Mariotta Cuthbertson * Mark Bos * Mark Dilks * Mark Norton * Mark Rogers * Martin Lockyer * Mary Masaba * Melanie Wellard * Michala Johnson * Michelle Francis * Michelle Hurst * Michelle Stewart * Michelle Trowman * Mike James * Mike Lewis * Milly Hayward * Maureen Gill-Beedie * Monica Porter * Naz Khan * Nichola Kingsbury * Nick Finney * Nicola Howell * Nicola Jayne Parker * Nicola Whaley * Nikky Briggs * Nobumi Kobayashi * Norman Hill * Patrick Rooney * Paul Limb *

Paul Underwood * Paula Tongs-Ketteringham * Paulette Cato-Tyson * Pauline Lawson * Penelope Chamberlain * Persephone Ward * Philippa Mathewson * Rachel Graham * Rachel Woodward Carrick * Chen Dawson * Richard Latteman * Richard Nugent * Richard Shorter * Richard Thomas * RKJ Adams * Rob Begg * Rob Oyston * Rob Pickering * Robert Lewis * Robyn Morrison * Rollo Maughfling * Rosalyn Spencer * Rosanna Mcinerney * Rosee Elliott * Rosie Godfrey * Roy Washington * Ruth Hayes * Ruth McDonagh * Ruthy Jowett * Sally Nesbitt * Sally Bezant * Sally Measom * Sally Rowe * Sam Forsberg * Sam Shepherd * Samantha Hawkins * Sandra White * Sarah Perks * Serban Nicolescu * Sharon Demiray * Sharon Sanders * Sharon Whatley * Sheila Starr * Sherry Lempka * Shindo Barquer * Si Sultan * Simon Dobinson * Sonja Byatt * Sophie Coddington * Speranza Holloway * Stefanie Lillie * Stella Lord * Steve Dobby * Steve Judge * Steve Kelly * Steve Scarlett * Steven Watson * Su Bailey * Sue Clarke * Sue Collinge * Sue Trusler * Susan Crichton * Susan Salmon * Suzanne Jane Howes * Suzanne Kemmenoe May * Suzanne Mitchell * Tanith Knox * Ted Swindale * Teresa Cripps * Theresa Jauregui * Tim Watts * Toby Philpott * Tracy McGlynn * Tricia Frances deGray * Vanessa Holmes * Vanessa Nichols * Vicky Fletcher * Victoria Pilling * Wendy McCracken * Wendy Phillips

The brilliant **Write That Book Masters** who freely shared their knowledge and expertise: Sara Cox, Tom Palmer, Katherine Clements, Paulo Delgado, Will Heather, Fiona Deal, Paul McGee, Catherine Emmett, Penny Haslam, Andy Bounds, Sue Richardson, Rory Scarfe, Alfie Joey, Natalie Kontarski, Eloise Cook, Rachel Kenny, Chris Cudmore, Mike Alden, Paul Mort, Grant Marshall and Paul East.

TEAM17 for being the most amazing online coaching community.

And you for buying and reading ***Write That Book***.

How We Can Help You

Please join our online communities. You'll receive support and the latest information about courses, talks and events. It's the very best way to connect with other authors who want to Write That Book.

Work directly with Michael Heppell or a Write That Book Coach.

If you would like to work with us, need a speaker for an event or would like information about one-to-one coaching.

If you'd like some guidance, or to find an expert to help you with your book, you can feel confident by contacting our trusted partners.

Information on all of the above can be found at:

www.WriteThatBook.co.uk

Other Books by Michael Heppell

How to Be Brilliant

Fed up of doing the same old things day in, day out? Tired of working hard for average results? Have the feeling that you could do more, be more?

How to Be Brilliant has been helping people enjoy brilliance for ten years. This international best-seller shows you how to make the critical steps from average to good and from good to brilliant - at work and in life. It'll help you work out what's happening right now and be clearer on how it could be so much better.

Then you'll be given strategies and powerful methods to help you get there:

- ·as quickly as possible
- ·as economically as possible
- ·with as much fun as possible

And once you know the secrets to being brilliant you can apply them to all areas of your life.

Don't be good. Be Brilliant.

5 Star Service

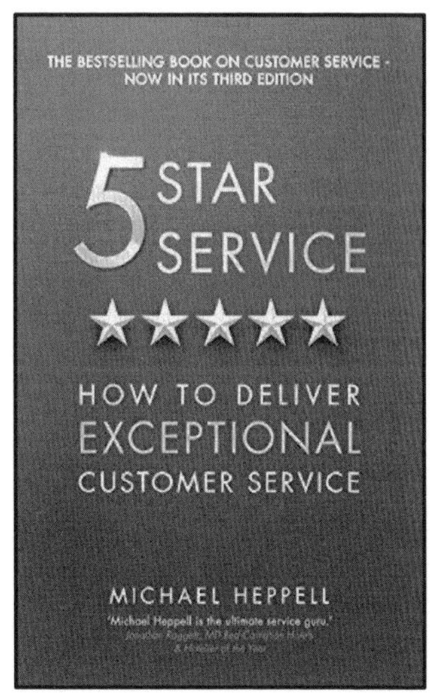

Create magic moments that will get you noticed, remembered and referred.

Nail the competitive edge that will knock out your customers and make your business stand out from the crowd. Watch as your positive reviews, rankings and reputation skyrocket. Discover how, with even the smallest of budgets you can:

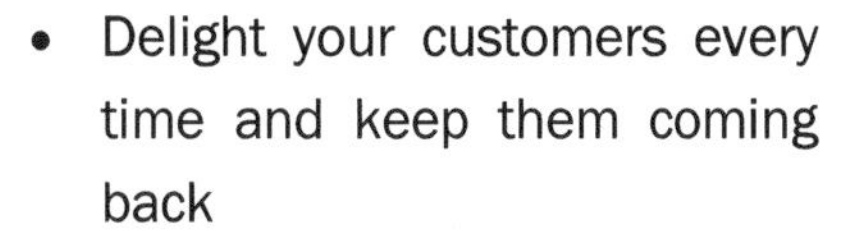

- Delight your customers every time and keep them coming back
- Win ever more customers without spending a fortune
- Get repeat orders and referrals from everyone you encounter
- Boost your profile, ranking and star-rating on online review sites
- Convert more enquiries into cash

In this third edition, you'll find over a dozen of Michael's brand new, best-ever techniques as well as all the winning strategies and case studies that have already made this one of the UK's most in-demand guides to first-class customer service.

Brilliant Life

Do you want to live life to the full? To know in years to come that you really gave it your all - and got the most out of your life?

The simplest way to a brilliant life is by making sure you're paying attention to what matters, in every area of your life. By making positive and lasting change where it's needed, when it's needed.

It's too easy to get swept along by the flow and then wonder what happened. We all need a bit of help to make sure we're living our best possible life. And that's where this book comes in.

Taking each area of your life by the horns, you'll quickly start to see what's working well and where attention is needed. One small action at a time, you'll move towards your own Brilliant Life.

STOP LIVING AN ORDINARY LIFE
START LIVING A BRILLIANT LIFE

Flip It *how to get the best out of everything*

The Sunday Times Number One Best-seller

There's a simple way of thinking, acting and doing that, once learned, will make sure you get the very best out of everything.

This book challenges you to get curious about how you interpret and handle every situation.

It liberates you from the beliefs that have been holding you back and gives you powerfully simple ways to switch your thinking. Change your actions so that you can get the very best from whatever life sends your way.

With the new, revised edition of this best-selling book, you'll discover how to make sure you never have a 'bad day' ever again.

How to Save an Hour Every Day

Would you like an extra hour a day, every day of your life, to do whatever you want with?

If this sounds like an impossible dream, then here's the good news: that extra hour really can be yours!

If you are willing to invest just an hour of your time to read it, choose the ideas that leap out to you and put them into action, you'll create extra time every single day, in a way you wouldn't believe could be possible.

You will:

- overcome procrastination and make better, faster decisions
- unearth hidden time for you - time to do the important things
- discover powerful new ways to organise your time and your life
- find out how to deal with the deadly 'time sappers'
- streamline and simplify absolutely everything you do - both at work and at home

We guarantee you'll find more time every day. What you do with it is up to you . . .

The Edge *how the best get better*

The very best didn't get there by accident. The best have a different way of thinking and acting in their daily lives.

And it's not enough to just succeed - they also have an uncontrollable desire - the desire to get better. The good news for the rest of us is that success leaves tracks. We only need to follow them.

Michael Heppell has spent his life studying successful people, attempting to distil what it is that the very best do that others don't.

He's interviewed entrepreneurs, personalities and leaders from politics to education. He's studied the daily habits of the elite and during this time he's uncovered what they do that gives them 'The Edge'.

By identifying and distilling this knowledge, you'll discover how you can use this same insight.

It's time to find your Edge.

17 the little way to get a lot done

With *17* you'll increase your productivity, wipe out wasted time, live your best life and accomplish more than you ever thought possible.

Use *17* to create, motivate and accelerate.

17 will give you new ways of thinking, acting and being, to live a more productive, wonderful and enjoyable life.

About the Author

Michael Heppell is the International Best-Selling author of 9 books. His personal development and business books have been published in 29 languages and are available in over 80 countries.

Michael is a popular keynote speaker who's been described as one of the top three professional speakers in the world.

As a coach, he's helped everyone from TV presenters to Premiership footballers, new authors to seasoned professionals.

In 2020 he launched Write That Book with a goal to help 1,000 new authors to write 1,000 books.

He lives in Northumberland, UK with his wife, co-author and business partner Christine.

www.MichaelHeppell.com

Write That Book